RHYMING IN THE RIGGING

POEMS OF THE SEA

RHYMING IN THE RIGGING

POEMS OF THE SEA

Edited by
Lahaina Harry

OX BOW PRESS
WOODBRIDGE, CT 06525

Acknowledgements

"Once by the Pacific" by Robert Frost from *The Poetry of Robert Frost* edited by Edward Connery Lathem. Copyright 1928, © 1969 by Holt, Rinehart and Winston. Copyright © 1956 by Robert Frost. Reprinted by permission of Holt, Rinehart and Winston, Publishers.

"The Pacific" in *A Fifth Avenue Parade and Other Poems* by Percy Stickney Grant. Copyright, 1922 by Percy Stickney Grant. By permission of Harper and Row, Publishers, Inc.

"The Sea Gypsy" by Richard Hovey from *Songs of Vagabondia* by Bliss Carman and Richard Hovey. By permission of Dodd, Mead & Company Inc., Publishers.

"The Main Sheet Song" by Thomas Fleming Day by permission of SEA Combined with Rudder.

"Exiled" and "Low Tide" by Edna St. Vincent Millay from *Collected Poems*, Harper and Row. Copyright 1921, 1949 by Edna St. Vincent Millay. Reprinted by permission of Norma Millay Ellis.

"A Sailor's Song" by Hazel Harper Harris. Reprinted by permission from The Christian Science Monitor.

"Tides" by A.G. Prys-Jones by permission of Basil Blackwell, Publisher.

"Song of the Sea" by Richard Burton from *The Collected Poems of Richard Burton*, Copyright 1931, R. 1959. Reprinted by permission of the Bobbs-Merrill Co., Inc.

"Boats in a Fog" by Robinson Jeffers. Copyright 1938 and renewed 1966 by Donnan Jeffers and Garth Jeffers. Reprinted from *The Selected Poetry of Robinson Jeffers*. Reprinted by permission of Random House, Inc.

"The Sailor to His Parrot" by W.H. Davies. Copyright © 1963 by Jonathan Cape Ltd. Reprinted from *The Complete Poems of W.H. Davies*, by permission of Wesleyan University Press.

"The Gulf Stream" by Henry Bellamann from *The Upward Pass*, and "The Fisherman" by Abbie Farwell Brown from *The Song of Sixpence*. Reprinted by permission of Houghton Mifflin Company

"Columbus" by Ogden Nash from *The Face is Familiar* by Ogden Nash, copyright 1935 by Ogden Nash, by permission of Little, Brown and Co.

Eleanore Myers Jewett, "Down Among the Wharves," St. Nicolas Magazine © 1922 renewed. Cale Young Rice, "Nights on the Indian Ocean" in *Sea Poems*. "The Sea King" by L. Frank Tooker. By permission of Prentice-Hall Inc. Englewood Cliffs, New Jersey

"They Who Possess the Sea" by Marguerite J. Adams of Sept. 30, 1943. © 1943 by the New York Times Company. Reprinted by permission.

"Sea Fever" by John Masefield from *Salt Water Poems and Ballads*. Copyright 1912 by Macmillan Publishing Co. Inc., renewed 1940 by John Masefield. "Hell's Pavement," "A Valediction," "A Wanderer's Song," "The Tarry Buccaneer," and "The Ship and Her Makers" by John Masefield from *Salt-Water Poems and Ballads*. Copyright 1916 by John Masefield, renewed 1944 by John Masefield. "Beautiful Proud Sea" by Sara Teasdale from *Collected Poems*. Copyright 1926 by Macmillan Publishing Co., Inc., renewed 1954 by Mamie T. Wheles. Reprinted with permission of Macmillan.

"Thornton Beach" Michael McClure, *Antechamber and Other Poems* Copyright © 1978 by Michael McClure. Reprinted by permission of New Directions Publishing Corporation.

ISBN: 0-918024-04-8
Library of Congress Card Number: 77-80048

Printed in the United States of America

To *'They that go down to the sea in ships'*

Psalm CVII

SEA-FEVER

I must down to the seas again, to the lonely sea and the sky,
And all I ask is a tall ship and a star to steer her by,
And the wheel's kick and the wind's song and the white
    sail's shaking,
And a grey mist on the sea's face and a grey dawn breaking.

I must down to the seas again, for the call of the running tide
Is a wild call and a clear call that may not be denied;
And all I ask is a windy day with the white clouds flying,
And the flung spray and the blown spume, and the
    sea-gulls crying.

I must down to the seas again to the vagrant gypsy life,
To the gull's way and the whale's way where the wind's like
    a whetted knife;
And all I ask is a merry yarn from a laughing fellow-rover,
And quiet sleep and a sweet dream when the long trick's
    over.

John Masefield

COLUMBUS

Behind him lay the gray Azores,
  Behind the Gates of Hercules;
Before him not the ghost of shores,
  Before him only shoreless seas.
The good mate said: "Now must we pray,
  For lo! the very stars are gone.
Speak, Admiral, speak, what shall I say?"
  "Why say, 'Sail on! sail on! and on!' "

"My men grow mutinous day by day;
  My men grow ghastly wan and weak."
The stout mate thought of home; a spray
  Of salt wave washed his swarthy cheek.
"What shall I say, brave Admiral, say,
  If we sight naught but seas at dawn?"
"Why, you shall say at break of day,
  'Sail on! sail on! sail on! and on!' "

They sailed and sailed, as winds might blow,
  Until at last the blanched mate said:
"Why, now not even God would know
  Should I and all my men fall dead.
These very winds forget their way,
  For God from these dread seas is gone.
Now speak, brave Admiral, speak and say—"
  He said: "Sail on! sail on! and on!"

They sailed. They sailed. Then spake the mate:
  "This mad sea shows his teeth to-night.
He curls his lip, he lies in wait,
  With lifted teeth, as if to bite!
Brave Admiral, say but one good word:
  What shall we do when hope is gone?"
The words leapt, as a leaping sword:
  "Sail on! sail on! sail on! and on!"

Then, pale and worn, he kept his deck,
    And peered through darkness. Ah, that night
Of all dark nights! And then a speck—
    A light! A light! A light! A light!
It grew, a star-lit flag unfurled!
    It grew to be Time's burst of dawn.
He gained a world! he gave that world
    Its grandest lesson: "On! sail on!"

Joaquin Miller

LOOMINGS

Whenever I find myself
growing grim about the mouth;
whenever it is a damp drizzly November
in my soul;
whenever I find myself involuntarily
pausing before coffin warehouses,
and bringing up the rear
of every funeral I meet;
and especially when my hypos
get such an upper hand of me,
that it requires a strong moral principle
to prevent me from deliberately
stepping into the street,
and methodically knocking people's hats off—
then, I account it high time
to get to sea
as soon as I can.
This is my substitute
for pistol and ball.
With a philosophical flourish
Cato throws himself upon his sword,
I quietly take to the ship.
There is nothing surprising in this.
If they but knew it,
almost all men in their degree,
some time or other,
cherish very nearly the same feelings
toward the ocean with me.

*From **Moby Dick**, Herman Melville*

A LIFE ON THE OCEAN WAVE

A life on the ocean wave,
  A home on the rolling deep,
Where the scattered waters rave,
  And the winds their revels keep:
Like an eagle caged, I pine
  On this dull, unchanging shore:
Oh! give me the flashing brine,
  The spray and the tempest's roar!

Once more on the deck I stand
  Of my own swift-gliding craft:
Set sail! farewell to the land!
  The gale follows fair abaft.
We shoot through the sparkling foam
  Like an ocean-bird set free;—
Like the ocean-bird, our home
  We'll find far out on the sea.

The land is no longer in view,
  The clouds have begun to frown;
But with a stout vessel and crew,
  We'll say, Let the storm come down!
And the song of our hearts shall be,
  While the winds and the waters rave,
A home on the rolling sea!
  A life on the ocean wave!

Epes Sargent

A WET SHEET AND A FLOWING SEA

A wet sheet and a flowing sea,
　A wind that follows fast,
And fills the white and rustling sail
　And bends the gallant mast;
And bends the gallant mast, my boys,
　While, like the eagle free,
Away the good ship flies, and leaves
　Old England on the lee.

O for a soft and gentle wind!
　I heard a fair one cry;
But give to me the snoring breeze
　And white waves heaving high;
And white waves heaving high, my lads,
　The good ship tight and free—
The world of waters is our home,
　And merry men are we.

There's tempest in yon horned moon,
　And lightning in yon cloud;
But hark the music, mariners!
　The wind is piping loud;
The wind is piping loud, my boys,
　The lightning flashes free—
While the hollow oak our palace is,
　Our heritage the sea.

Allan Cunningham

THE SEA GYPSY

I am fevered with the sunset,
I am fretful with the bay,
For the wander-thirst is on me
And my soul is in Cathay.

There's a schooner in the offing,
With her topsails shot with fire,
And my heart has gone aboard her
For the Islands of Desire.

I must forth again tomorrow!
With the sunset I must be
Hull down on the trail of rapture
In the wonder of the Sea.

Richard Hovey

O CAPTAIN! MY CAPTAIN!

O Captain! my Captain! our fearful trip is done,
The ship has weathered every rack, the prize we sought
is won,
The port is near, the bells I hear, the people all exulting,
While follow eyes the steady keel, the vessel grim and
daring;
But, O heart! heart! heart!
O the bleeding drops of red,
Where on the deck my Captain lies,
Fallen cold and dead.

O Captain! my Captain! rise up and hear the bells;
Rise up—for you the flag is flung—for you the bugle trills,
For you bouquets and ribboned wreaths—for you the
shores a-crowding,
For you they call, the swaying mass, their eager faces
turning;
Here Captain! dear father!
This arm beneath your head!
It is some dream that on the deck
You've fallen cold and dead.

My Captain does not answer, his lips are pale and still,
My father does not feel my arm, he has no pulse nor will,
The ship is anchored safe and sound, its voyage closed and
done,
From fearful trip the victor ship comes in with object won;
Exult, O shores, and ring, O bells!
But I, with mournful tread,
Walk the deck my Captain lies,
Fallen cold and dead.

Walt Whitman

THE LIFE OF A TAR

The life of a tar is the life I love;
The sea is beneath us, the heavens above;
Our reign undisputed from the sky to the sea,
Whose life can compare to the mariner free;
When winds whistle loud, still in safety we ride,
Through waves which ne'er whelm as we merrily ride,
No life half so happy, no life half so free,
While we skim undismay'd o'er the rolling sea.

The hope of our maidens, the pride of our isle,
His heart is a stranger to falsehood and guile;
His ship is his home, his nation the world,
His boast is his flag, never wrongly unfurl'd;
His heart his true honour—how happy is he,
While he skims undismay'd o'er the rolling sea,
No life half so happy, no life half so free,
While we skim undismay'd o'er the rolling sea.

Anonymous

THE MAIN-SHEET SONG

Rushing along on a narrow reach,
  Our rival under the lee,
The wind falls foul of the weather leach,
  And the jib flaps fretfully.
The skipper casts a glance along,
  And handles his wheel to meet—
Then sings in the voice of a stormy song,
  "All hands get on that sheet!"

Yo ha! Yo ho! Then give her a spill
  With a rattle of blocks abaft.
Yo ha! Yo ho! Come down with a will
  And bring the main-sheet aft.

Rolling the foam up over the rail
  She smokes along and flings
A spurt of spray in the curving sail,
  And plunges and rolls and springs;
For a wild, wet spot is the scuppers' sweep,
  As we stand to our knees along—
It's a foot to make and a foot to keep
  As we surge to the bullie's song.

Yo ha! Yo ho! Then give her a spill
  With a rattle of blocks abaft.
Yo ha! Yo ho! Come down with a will
  And bring the main-sheet aft.

Muscle and mind are a winning pair
  With a lively plank below,
That whether the wind be foul or fair
  Will pick up her heels and go;
For old hemp and hands are shipmates long—
  There's work whenever they meet—
So here's to a pull that's steady and strong,
  When all hands get on the sheet.

Yo ha! Yo ho! Then give her a spill
   With a rattle of blocks abaft.
Yo ha! Yo ho! Come down with a will
   And bring the main-sheet aft.

Thomas Fleming Day

SPIRIT OF FREEDOM, THOU DOST LOVE THE SEA

Spirit of freedom, thou dost love the sea,
Trackless and storm-tost ocean wild and free,
Faint symbol of thine own eternity.
   The seagulls wheel and soar and fearless roam,
   The stormy petrel dashes through the foam;
The mighty billows heave, the tempests roar,
The diapason thunders shake the shore
And chant the song of freedom evermore.

Henry Nehemiah Dodge

THE FISHER'S LIFE

What joy attends the fisher's life!
    Blow, windo, blow!
The fisher and his faithful wife!
    Row, boys, row!
He drives no plough on stubborn land,
His fields are ready to his hand;
No nipping frosts his orchards fear,
He has his autumn all the year!

The husbandman has rent to pay,
    Blow, winds, blow!
And seed to purchase every day,
    Row, boys, row!
But he who farms the rolling deeps,
Though never sowing, always reaps;
The ocean's fields are fair and free,
There are no rent days on the sea!

Anonymous

SONG FROM 'THE TEMPEST'

The Master, the Swabber, the Boat-swain and I;
The Gunner, and his Mate,
Lov'd Mall, Meg, and Marrian, and Margery,
But none of us car'd for Kate,
For she had a tongue with a tang,
Would cry to a Sailour go hang:
She lov'd not the savour of Tar nor of Pitch,
 Yet a Taylor might scratch her where ere she did itch.
 Then to Sea Boys, and let her go hang.

William Shakespeare

A SAILOR'S SONG

As I sail home to Galveston
In oleander time,
I sing a chanty of the sea,
A swinging seaman's rhyme;
And tell the wind to wing my words
Across the churning foam
To let my own dear folk rejoice
That I am coming home.

Although I love the rolling keel,
The waves, and briny spray,
The Gulf is bluer far to me
Than Naples' cobalt bay;
And yearningly I face the west
Dyed orange, plum, and lime,
As I sail home to Galveston
In oleander time.

Salt cedars will be feathered pink,
And every humble street
Will flaunt the coral, rose, and white
Of oleanders sweet.
What joy my heart anticipates
In this sea-girdled clime
As I sail home to Galveston
In oleander time!

Hazel Harper Harris

OLD IRONSIDES

Ay, tear her tattered ensign down!
　　Long has it waved on high,
And many an eye has danced to see
　　That banner in the sky;
Beneath it rung the battle shout,
　　And burst the cannon's roar;—
The meteor of the ocean air
　　Shall sweep the clouds no more.

Her deck, once red with heroes' blood,
　　Where knelt the vanquished foe,
When winds were hurrying o'er the flood,
　　And waves were white below,
No more shall feel the victor's tread,
　　Or know the conquered knee;
The harpies of the shore shall pluck
　　The eagle of the sea!

Oh, better that her shattered hulk
　　Should sink beneath the wave!
Her thunders shook the mighty deep,
　　And there should be her grave;
Nail to the mast her holy flag,
　　Set every threadbare sail,
And give her to the god of storms,
　　The lightning, and the gale!

Oliver Wendell Holmes

REEFING TOPSAILS

Three hand-spike raps on the forward hatch,
  A hoarse voice shouts down the fo'castle dim,
Startling the sleeping starboard watch,
  Out of their bunks, their clothes to snatch,
    With little thought of life or limb.

"All hands on deck! d'ye hear the news?
  Reef topsails all—'tis the old man's word.
Tumble up, never mind jackets or shoes!"
Never a man would dare refuse,
  When that stirring cry is heard.

The weather shrouds are like iron bars,
  The leeward backstays curving out.
Like steely spear-points gleam the stars
From the black sky flecked with feathery bars,
  By the storm-wind swerved about.

Across the bows like a sheeted ghost,
  Quivers a luminous cloud of spray,
Flooding the forward deck, and most
Of the waist; then, like a charging host,
  It rolls to leeward away.

"Mizzen topsail, clew up and furl;
  Clew up your main course now with a will!"
The wheel goes down with a sudden whirl.
"Ease her, ease her, the good old girl,
  Don't let your head sails fill!"

"Ease off lee braces; round in on the weather;
  Ease your halyards; clew down, clew down;
Haul out your reef tackles, now together!"
Like an angry bull against his tether,
  Heave the folds of the topsails brown.

"Haul taut your buntlines, cheerly, men, now!"
   The gale sweeps down with a fiercer shriek,
Shock after shock on the weather bow
Thunders the head sea, and below
   Throbbing timbers groan and creak.

The topsail yards are down on the caps;
   Her head lies up in the eyes of the blast;
The bellying sails, with sudden slaps,
Swell out and angrily collapse,
   Shaking the head of the springing mast.

Wilder and heavier comes the gale
   Out of the heart of the Northern Sea;
And the phosphorescent gleamings pale
Surge up awash of the monkey rail
   Along our down pressed lee.

"Lay aloft! lay aloft, boys, and reef,
   Don't let my starbolines be last,"
Cries from the deck the sturdy chief;
"Twill take a man of muscle and beef
   To get those ear-rings passed!"

Into the rigging with a shout,
   Our second and third mates foremost spring;
Crackles the ice on the ratlines stout,
As the leaders on the yards lay out,
   And the footropes sway and swing.

On the weather end of the jumping yard,
   One hand on the lift, and one beneath,
Grasping the cringle, and tugging hard,
Black Dan, our third, grim and scarred,
   Clutches the ear-ring for life or death.

"Light up to windward!" cries the mate,
    As he rides the surging yardarm end;
And into the work we throw our weight,
Every man bound to emulate,
    The rush of the gale, and the sea's wild send.

"Haul out to leeward," comes at last,
    With a cheering from the fore and main;
"Knot your reef-points, and knot them fast!"
Weather and lee are the ear-rings passed,
    And over the yard we bend and strain.

"Lay down men, all; and now with a will,
    Swing on your topsail halyards, and sway;
Ease your braces and let her fill,
There's an hour below of the mid-watch still,
    Haul taut your bowlines—well all—belay!"

Walter Mitchell

CROSSING THE BAR

Sunset and evening star,
  And one clear call for me!
And may there be no moaning of the bar,
  When I put out to sea,

But such a tide as moving seems asleep,
  Too full for sound and foam,
When that which drew from out the boundless deep
  Turns again home.

Twilight and evening bell,
  And after that the dark!
And may there be no sadness of farewell,
  When I embark.

For tho' from out our bourne of Time and Place
  The flood may bear me far,
I hope to see my Pilot face to face
  When I have crossed the bar.

Alfred Tennyson

IF I COULD GRASP A WAVE FROM THE GREAT SEA

If I could grasp a wave from the great sea,
Mold it a precious stone of faultless blue,
And with a lapidary's art could hew
Away each useless fragment skillfully,
The beauty its pellucid depths would hold
Of molten fire and agony of ice,
Of storm and calm, of love and sacrifice,
Would make a gem whose splendor none has told.

The sea has mirrored all known loveliness
Of sun and moon and stars, of day and night,
Of terror and the wind—the mystery
Of Aphrodite, born of the waves' caress;
And more than these, that flame holy and white,
The face of Him who walked on Galilee.

John Richard Moreland

THE FISHERMAN

The fisherman goes out at dawn
  When everyone's abed,
And from the bottom of the sea
  Draws up his daily bread.

His life is strange; half on the shore
  And half upon the sea—
Not quite a fish, and yet not quite
  The same as you and me.

The fisherman has curious eyes,
  They make you feel so queer,
As if they had seen many things
  Of wonder and of fear.

They're like the wondrous tales he tells—
  Not gray, nor yet quite blue;
They're like the wondrous tales he tells—
  Not quite—yet maybe—true.

He knows so much of boats and tides,
  Of winds and clouds and sky!
But when I tell of city things,
  He sniffs and shuts one eye!

Abbie Farwell Brown

ANNABEL LEE

It was many and many a year ago,
  In a kingdom by the sea,
That a maiden there lived whom you may know
  By the name of Annabel Lee;
And this maiden she lived with no other thought
  Than to love and be loved by me.

I was a child and she was a child,
  In this kingdom by the sea,
But we loved with a love that was more than love,
  I and my Annabel Lee;
With a love that the winged seraphs of heaven
  Coveted her and me.

And this was the reason that, long ago,
  In this kingdom by the sea,
A wind blew out of a cloud, chilling
  My beautiful Annabel Lee;
So that her highborn kinsmen came
  And bore her away from me,
To shut her up in a sepulchre
  In this kingdom by the sea.

The angels, not half so happy in heaven,
  Went envying her and me;
Yes! that was the reason (as all men know,
  In this kingdom by the sea)
That the wind came out of the cloud by night,
  Chilling and killing my Annabel Lee.

But our love it was stronger by far than the love
  Of those who were older than we,
  Of many far wiser than we;
And neither the angels in heaven above,
  Nor the demons down under the sea,
Can ever dissever my soul from the soul
  Of the beautiful Annabel Lee:

For the moon never beams, without bringing me dreams
  Of the beautiful Annabel Lee,
And the stars never rise, but I feel the bright eyes
  Of the beautiful Annabel Lee;
And so, all the night-tide, I lie down by the side
Of my darling—my darling—my life and my bride,
  In her sepulchre there by the sea,
  In her tomb by the sounding sea.

                                        Edgar Allan Poe

THE SECRET OF THE SEA

Ah! what pleasant visions haunt me
   As I gaze upon the sea!
All the old romantic legends,
   All my dreams, come back to me.

Sails of silk and ropes of sandal,
   Such as gleam in ancient lore;
And the singing of the sailors,
   And the answer from the shore!

Most of all, the Spanish ballad
   Haunts me oft, and tarries long,
Of the noble Count Arnaldos
   And the sailor's mystic song.

Like the long waves on a sea-beach,
   Where the sand as silver shines,
With a soft, monotonous cadence,
   Flow its unrhymed lyric lines;—

Telling how the Count Arnaldos,
   With his hawk upon his hand,
Saw a fair and stately galley,
   Steering onward to the land;—

How he heard the ancient helmsman
   Chant a song so wild and clear,
That the sailing sea-bird slowly
   Poised upon the mast to hear,

Till his soul was full of longing
   And he cried, with impulse strong,—
"Helmsman! for the love of heaven,
   Teach me, too, that wondrous song!"

"Wouldst thou,"—so the helmsman answered,
   "Learn the secret of the sea?
Only those who brave its dangers
   Comprehend its mystery!"

In each sail that skims the horizon,
   In each landward-blowing breeze,
I behold that stately galley,
   Hear those mournful melodies;

Till my soul is full of longing
   For the secret of the sea,
And the heart of the great ocean
   Sends a thrilling pulse through me.

Henry Wadsworth Longfellow

MY BOUNDING BARK

My bounding bark, I fly to thee,
   I'm wearied of the shore,
I long to hail the swelling sea,
   And wander free once more.
A sailor's life of reckless glee,
That only is the life for me.

I was not born for fashion's slave,
   Or the dull city's strife;
Be mine the spirit-stirring wave,
   And roving sailor's life.
A life of freedom on the sea,
That only is the life for me.

I was not born for lighted halls,
   Or the gay revels round,
My music is where Ocean calls,
   And echoing rocks resound.
The wandering sailor's life of glee,
That only is the life for me.

Anonymous

THE DEEP

There's beauty in the deep;
The wave is bluer than the sky;
And though the lights shine bright on high,
More softly do the sea-gems glow
That sparkle in the depths below;
The rainbow's tints are only made
When on the waters they are laid,
And Sun and Moon most sweetly shine
Upon the ocean's level brine.
There's beauty in the deep.

There's music in the deep:—
It is not in the surf's rough roar,
Nor in the whispering, shelly shore—
They are but earthly sounds, that tell
How little of the sea nymph's shell,
That sends its loud, clear note abroad,
Or winds its softness through the flood,
Echoes through groves with coral gay,
And dies, on spongy banks, away.
There's music in the deep.

There's quiet in the deep:—
Above, let tides and tempests rave,
And earth-born whirlwinds wake the wave;
Above, let care and fear contend,
With sin and sorrow to the end;
Here, far beneath the tainted foam,
That frets above our peaceful home,
We dream in joy, and wake in love,
Nor know the rage that yells above.
There's quiet in the deep.

John G.C. Brainard

THE SHIP OF STATE

Sail on, sail on, O Ship of State!
Sail on, O Union, strong and great!
Humanity, with all its fears,
With all the hopes of future years,
Is hanging breathless on thy fate!
We know what Master laid thy keel,
What Workmen wrought thy ribs of steel,
Who made each mast, and sail, and rope,
What anvils rang, what hammers beat,
In what a forge and what a heat
Were shaped the anchors of thy hope!
Fear not each sudden sound and shock—
'Tis of the wave, and not the rock;
'Tis but the flapping of the sail,
And not a rent made by the gale!
In spite of rock and tempest roar,
In spite of false lights on the shore,
Sail on, nor fear to breast the sea!
Our hearts, our hopes, are all with thee.
Our hearts, our hopes, our prayers, our tears,
Our faith, triumphant o'er our fears,
Are all with thee, are all with thee!

Henry Wadsworth Longfellow

EXILED

Searching my heart for its true sorrow,
  This is the thing I find to be:
That I am weary of words and people,
  Sick of the city, wanting the sea;

Wanting the sticky, salty sweetness
  Of the strong wind and shattered spray;
Wanting the loud sound and the soft sound
  Of the big surf that breaks all day.

Always before about my dooryard,
  Marking the reach of the winter sea,
Rooted in sand and dragging drift-wood,
  Straggled the purple wild sweet-pea;

Always I climbed the wave at morning,
  Shook the sand from my shoes at night,
That now am caught beneath great buildings,
  Stricken with noise, confused with light.

If I could hear the green piles groaning
  Under the windy wooden piers,
See once again the bobbing barrels,
  And the black sticks that fence the weirs,

If I could see the weedy mussels
  Crusting the wrecked and rotting hulls,
Hear once again the hungry crying
  Overhead, of the wheeling gulls,

Feel once again the shanty straining
  Under the turning of the tide,
Fear once again the rising freshet,
  Dread the bell in the fog outside,

I should be happy,—that was happy
    All day long on the coast of Maine!
I have a need to hold and handle
    Shells and anchors and ships again!

I should be happy, that am happy
    Never at all since I came here.
I am too long away from water.
    I have a need of water near.

                    Edna St. Vincent Millay

THE WALLOPING WINDOW-BLIND

A capital ship for an ocean trip
   Was the "Walloping Window blind"
No gale that blew dismayed her crew
   Or troubled the captain's mind.
The man at the wheel was taught to feel
   Contempt for the wildest blow,
And it often appeared, when the weather had cleared,
   That he'd been in his bunk below.

The boatswain's mate was very sedate,
   Yet fond of amusement, too;
And he played hop-scotch with the starboard watch,
   While the captain tickled the crew.
And the gunner we had was apparently mad,
   For he sat on the after rail,
And fired salutes with the captain's boots,
   In the teeth of the booming gale.

The captain sat in a commodore's hat
   And dined in a royal way
On toasted pigs and pickles and figs
   And gummery bread each day.
But the cook was Dutch and behaved as such:
   For the food that he gave the crew
Was a number of tons of hot-cross buns
   Chopped up with sugar and glue.

And we all felt ill as mariners will,
   On a diet that's cheap and rude;
And we shivered and shook as we dipped the cook
   In a tub of his gluesome food.
Then nautical pride we laid aside,
   And we cast the vessel ashore
On the Gulliby Isles, where the Poohpooh smiles,
   And the Anagazanders roar.

Composed of sand was that favored land,
    And trimmed with cinnamon straws;
And pink and blue was the pleasing hue
    Of the Tickletoeteaser's claws.
And we sat on the edge of a sandy ledge
    And shot at the whistling bee;
And the Binnacle-bats wore water-proof hats
    As they danced in the sounding sea.

On rubagub bark, from dawn to dark,
    We fed, till we all had grown
Uncommonly shrunk,—when a Chinese junk
    Came by from the torriby zone.
She was stubby and square, but we didn't much care,
    And we cheerily put to sea;
And we left the crew of the junk to chew
    The bark of the rubagub tree.

Charles E. Carryl

UNFATHOMABLE SEA!

Unfathomable Sea! whose waves are years!
  Ocean of Time, whose waters of deep woe
Are brackish with the salt of human tears!
  Thou shoreless flood which in thy ebb and flow
Claspest the limits of mortality,
And, sick of prey, yet howling on for more,
Vomitest thy wrecks on its inhospitable shore!
Treacherous in calm, and terrible in storm,
  Who shall put forth on thee,
        Unfathomable Sea?

Percy Bysshe Shelley

A SEA DIRGE

Full fathom five thy father lies;
　Of his bones are coral made:
Those are pearls that were his eyes:
　Nothing of him that doth fade,
　But doth suffer a sea-change
　Into something rich and strange.
　Sea-nymphs hourly ring his knell.
　　　Ding-dong.
Hark! now I hear them,—ding-dong, bell.

　　　From **The Tempest,** *William Shakespeare*

MARINERS

Men who have loved the ships they took to sea,
  Loved the tall masts, the prows that creamed with foam,
Have learned, deep in their hearts, how it might be
  That there is yet a dearer thing than home.
The decks they walk, the rigging in the stars,
  The clean boards counted in the watch they keep—
These, and the sunlight on the slippery spars,
  Will haunt them ever, waking and asleep.

Ashore, these men are not as other men:
  They walk as strangers through the crowded street,
Or, brooding by their fires, they hear again
  The drone astern, where gurgling waters meet,
Or see again a wide and blue lagoon,
  And a lone ship that rides there with the moon.

David Morton

CASABIANCA

The boy stood on the burning deck,
  Whence all but him had fled;
The flame that lit the battle's wreck
  Shone round him o'er the dead.

Yet beautiful and bright he stood,
  As born to rule the storm;
A creature of heroic blood,
  A proud though childlike form.

The flames rolled on; he would not go
  Without his father's word;
That father, faint in death below,
  His voice no longer heard.

He called aloud, "Say, father, say,
  If yet my task be done?"
He knew not that the chieftain lay
  Unconscious of his son.

"Speak, father!" once again he cried,
  "If I may yet be gone!"
And but the booming shots replied,
  And fast the flames rolled on.

Upon his brow he felt their breath,
  And in his waving hair,
And looked from the lone post of death
  In still yet brave despair;

And shouted but once more aloud,
  "My father! must I stay?"
While o'er him fast, through sail and shroud,
  The wreathing fires made way.

They wrapt the ship in splendor wild,
  They caught the flag on high,
And streamed above the gallant child,
  Like banners in the sky.

There came a burst of thunder sound;
   The boy,—Oh! where was *he?*
Ask of the winds, that far around
   With fragments strewed the sea,—

With shroud and mast and pennon fair,
   That well had borne their part,—
But the noblest thing that perished there
   Was that young, faithful heart.

Felicia Hemans

THE CRUISE OF THE "P.C."

Across the swiffling waves they went,
　　The gumly bark yoked to and fro,
The jupple crew on pleasure bent,
　　Galored, "This is a go!"

Beside the poo's'l stood the Gom,
　　He chirked and murgled in his glee;
While near him, in a grue jipon,
　　The Bard was quite at sea.

"Gollop! Golloy! Thou scrumjous Bard!
　　Take pen (thy stylo) and endite
A pome, my brain needs kurgling hard,
　　And I will feast tonight."

That wansome Bard he took his pen,
　　A flirgly look around he guv;
He squoffled once, he squirled, and then
　　He wrote what's writ above.

Anonymous

AND GOD CREATED THE GREAT WHALES

And God created the great whales, and each
Soul living, each that crept, which plenteously
The waters generated by their kinds,
And every bird of wing after his kind;
And saw that it was good, and bless'd them, saying,
Be fruitful, multiply, and in the seas,
And lakes, and running streams, the waters fill;
And let the fowl be multiply'd on the earth.
Forthwith the sounds and seas, each creek and bay,
With fry innumerable swarm, and shoals
Of fish, that with their fins and shining scales
Glide under the green wave, in sculls that oft
Bank the mid sea: part single, or with mate,
Graze the sea weed their pasture, and through groves
Of coral stray, or sporting with quick glance
Show to the sun their wav'd coats dropt with gold;
Or in their pearly shells at ease attend
Moist nutriment, or under rocks their food
In jointed armor watch: on smooth the seal
And bended dolphins play; part huge of bulk,
Wallowing unwieldly, enormous in their gait,
Tempest the ocean; there Leviathan,
Hugest of living creatures, on the deep
Stretch'd like a promontory sleeps, or swims
And seems a moving land, and at his gills
Draws in, and at his trunk spouts out a sea.

*From **Paradise Lost,** John Milton*

FATHER MAPPLE'S HYMN

The ribs and terrors in the whale,
    Arched over me a dismal gloom,
While all God's sun-lit waves rolled by,
    And lift me deepening down to doom.

I saw the opening maw of hell,
    With endless pains and sorrows there;
Which none but they that feel can tell—
    Oh, I was plunging to despair.

In black distress, I called my God,
    When I could scarce believe him mine,
He bowed his ear to my complaints—
    No more the whale did me confine.

With speed he flew to my relief,
    As on a radiant dolphin borne;
Awful, yet bright, as lightning shone
    The face of my Deliverer God.

My song for ever shall record
    That terrible, that joyful hour;
I give the glory to my God,
    His all the mercy and the power.

From **Moby Dick**, *Herman Melville*

THE WHALE

" 'Tis a hundred years," said the bosun bold,
   "Since I was a boy at sea;
'Tis a hundred years, so I've been told,
   And that's the truth," said he.
"We sailed one day from Milford Bay,
   The North Pole for to see;
And we found it too, without much a-do,
   And that's the truth," said he.

"We sailed and sailed, and one fair noon
   A great whale we espied,
So we took a rope and a long harpoon,
   And stuck him in the starboard side.
Then away and away went the great big whale,
   And away and away went we:
Tied fast to his tail to the North we did sail,
   And that 's the truth," said he.

"And when we came to the great North Star
   An iceberg we did see.
Said the captain: 'Now we have come thus far,
   I am not going back,' said he.
So we tickled the tail of that great big whale
   With a tenpenny nail did we,
And we sailed right through that iceberg blue,
   And that's the truth," said he.

"And then the North Pole we did see,
   And we anchored the whale astern,
But he gave us a whack, that sent us back,
   Or I shouldn't have been spinning this yarn.
So messmates all" said the bosun bold,
   "If the North Pole you would see,
You've only got to sail at the tail of a whale,
   And that's the truth," said he.

Anonymous

THE OWL AND THE PUSSY-CAT

The Owl and the Pussy-Cat went to sea
   In a beautiful pea-green boat;
They took some honey and plenty of money
   Wrapped up in a five-pound note.

The Owl looked up to the stars above
   And sang to a small guitar;
"Oh, lovely Pussy, oh, Pussy, my love,
   What a beautiful Pussy you are!"

Pussy said to the Owl: "You elegant fowl,
   How charmingly sweetly you sing!
Oh, let us be married, too long have we tarried—
   But what shall we do for a ring?"

So they sailed away for a year and a day
   To the land where the bone-tree grows;
And there in a wood a piggy-wig stood,
   With a ring at the end of his nose.

"Dear Pig, are you willing to sell for one shilling
   Your ring?" Said the Piggy, "I will."
So they took it away and were married next day
   By the Turkey that lives on the hill.

They had apples and quince and piles of mince
   Which they ate with a silver spoon,
And hand in hand on the edge of the sand
   They danced by the light of the moon.

Edward Lear

THEY WHO POSSESS THE SEA

They who possess the sea within their blood
have blood that courses with an endless motion,
deep is its surging, like a tide at flood from out of the ocean.
They hold the blue spray-water in their veins
that hints no crimson torn from leaf or berry,
neither the flame of sumach nor the stain of the wild cherry.
To mariners the call of land is thinned
   to a reed's calling. They who know the sound
of surf have blood tempestuous as wind
   yet ever bound.

Marguerite Janvrin Adams

SHIPS THAT PASS IN THE NIGHT

Ships that pass in the night
  and speak each other in passing,
Only a signal shown
  and a distant voice in the darkness;
So on the ocean of life,
  we pass and speak one another,
Only a look and a voice,
  then darkness again and a silence.

Henry Wadsworth Longfellow

AN OCEAN LULLABY

Our ship is a cradle on ocean's blue billow;
Rest, little spirit, your head on your pillow!
Dream of the dolphin that leaps from the water,
Dream of the flying-fish, dear little daughter;
Dream of the tropic-bird, lone in his flight,—
Where is he sleeping, I wonder, tonight?
Dark is the water with white crests of foam;
Sleep, little mermaid, the sea is your home!
Stars in the heavens are twinkling past number;
Waters are whispering slumber, love, slumber;
Waves are a-murmuring sleep, dearest, sleep!—
And the little one slumbers in peace on the deep.
Sing away wavelets and sigh away low,
Winds of the tropics about us may blow;
Baby is sleeping and mother is singing
And the peace of the evening about us is winging.
Sleep, little mermaid, as onward we roam,
The ship is your cradle, the sea is your home.

Charles Keeler

THE SEA-KING'S BURIAL

"My strength is failing fast,"
  Said the sea-king to his men,
"I shall never sail the seas
  Like a conqueror again,
But while yet a drop remains
Of the life-blood in my veins,
Raise, oh, raise me from my bed;
Put the crown upon my head;
Put my good sword in my hand,
And so lead me to the strand,
  Where my ship at anchor rides
                Steadily;
If I cannot end my life
In the crimsoned battle-strife,
  Let me die as I have lived,
                On the sea."

They have raised King Balder up,
  Put his crown upon his head;
They have sheathed his limbs in mail,
  And the purple o'er him spread;
And amid the greeting rude
Of a gathering multitude,
Borne him slowly to the shore—
All the energy of yore
From his dim eyes flashing forth—
Old sea-lion of the North—
  As he looked upon his ship
                Riding free,
And on his forehead pale
Felt the cold, refreshing gale,
  And heard the welcome sound
                Of the sea.

They have borne him to the ship
　With a slow and solemn tread;
They have placed him on the deck
　With his crown upon his head,
Where he sat as on a throne:
And have left him there alone,
With his anchor ready weighed,
And his snowy sails displayed
To the favouring wind, once more
Blowing freshly from the shore,
　And have bidden him farewell
　　　　　　　　Tenderly,
Saying: "King of mighty men,
We shall meet thee yet again,
　In Valhalla, with the monarchs
　　　　　Of the sea."

Underneath him in the hold
　They had placed the lighted brand:
And the fire was burning slow
　As the vessel from the land,
Like a stag-hound from the slips,
Darted forth from out the ships.
There was music in her sail
As it swelled before the gale,
And a dashing at her prow
As it cleft the waves below;
　And the good ship sped along,
　　　　　　Scudding free;
As on many a battle morn
In her time she had been borne,
　To struggle, and to conquer
　　　　　On the sea.

And the king with sudden strength
　Started up, and paced the deck,
With his good sword for his staff,
　And his robe around his neck.
Once alone, he raised his hand
To the people on the land;
And with shout and joyous cry
Once again they made reply,
Till the loud, exulting cheer
Sounded faintly on his ear;
　　For the gale was o'er him blowing
　　　　　　　　Fresh and free;
And ere yet an hour had passed,
He was driven before the blast,
　And a storm was on his path,
　　　　　　　　On the sea.

"So blow, ye tempests, blow,
　And my spirit shall not quail;
I have fought with many a foe,
　I have weathered many a gale;
And in this hour of death,
Ere I yield my fleeting breath—
Ere the fire now burning slow
Shall come rushing from below,
And this worn and wasted frame
Be devoted to the flame—
　I will raise my voice in triumph,
　　　　　　　　Singing free;
To the great All-Father's home
I am driving through the foam,
　I am sailing to Valhalla,
　　　　　　　　O'er the sea.

"So blow, ye stormy winds—
   And ye flames, ascend on high;
In easy, idle bed
   Let the slave and coward die!
But give me the driving keel,
Clang of shields and flashing steel;
Or my foot on foreign ground,
With my enemies around!
Happy, happy, thus I'd yield,
On the deck or in the field,
   My last breath, shouting 'On
                     To victory.'
But since this has been denied,
They shall say that I have died
   Without flinching, like a monarch
                     Of the sea."

And Balder spoke no more,
   And no sound escaped his lip;
And he looked, yet scarcely saw
   The destruction of his ship,
Nor the fleet sparks mounting high,
Nor the glare upon the sky;
Scarcely heard the billows dash,
Nor the burning timber crash;
Scarcely felt the scorching heat
That was gathering at his feet,
   Nor the fierce flames mounting o'er him
                     Greedily,
But the life was in him yet,
And the courage to forget
   All his pain, in his triumph
                     On the sea.

Once alone, a cry arose,
  Half of anguish, half of pride,
As he sprang upon his feet,
  With the flames on every side.
"I am coming!" said the king,
"Where the swords and bucklers ring,
Where the warrior lives again,
Where the souls of mighty men,
Where the weary find repose,
And the red wine ever flows.
  I am coming, great All-Father,
                      Unto Thee!
Unto Odin, unto Thor,
And the strong, true hearts of yore—
  I am coming to Valhalla,
                      O'er the sea."

Charles Mackay

WHERE IS THE SEA?

Song of the Greek Islander in exile

A Greek Islander, being taken to the Vale of
Tempe, and called upon to admire its beauty,
only replied—*"The Sea–where is it?"*

Where is the sea?—I languish here—
   Where is my own blue sea?
With all its barks in fleet career,
   And flags, and breezes free.

I miss that voice of waves, which first
   Awoke my childhood's glee;
The measured chime—the thundering burst—
   Where is my own blue sea?

Oh! rich your myrtle's breath may rise,
   Soft, soft your winds may be;
Yet my sick heart within me dies—
   Where is my own blue sea?

I hear the shepherd's mountain flute—
   I hear the whispering trees;
The echoes of my soul are mute:
   —Where is my own blue sea?

Felicia Hemans

HURRAH FOR THE SEA

A bold, brave crew, on an ocean blue,
   And a ship that loves the blast,
With a good wind piping merrily
  In the tall and gallant mast.
    Ha! ha! my boys,
    These are the joys,
  Of the noble and the brave,
    Who love a life
    In the tempest's strife,
  And a home on the mountain wave.

When the driving rain of the hurricane,
  Puts the light of the lighthouse out,
And the growling thunder sound is going
  On the whirlwind's battle rout.
    Ha! ha! do you think,
    That the valiant shrink?
No! no! we are bold and brave,
  And we love to fight
In the wild midnight,
With the storm on the mountain wave.

Breezes that die where the green woods sigh,
  To the landsmen sweet may be,
But give to the brave the broad-backed wave,
  And the tempest's midnight glee!
    Ha! ha! the blast,
    And the rocking mast,
  And the sea wind brisk and cold,
    And the thunder's jar
    On the seas afar
  Are things that suit the bold.

The timbers creak, the sea birds shriek,
  There's lightning in the blast!
Hard to the leeward, mariners,
  For the storm is gathering fast.
    Ha! ha! to-night,
    Boys, we must fight;
  But the winds which o'er us yell,
    Shall never scare
    The mariner
  In his winged citadel.

Anonymous

DOWN AMONG THE WHARVES

Down among the wharves—that's the place I like to
  wander!
  Smell of tar and salted fish and barrels soaked in brine!
Here and there a lobster-crate, and brown seines over
  yonder,
    And in among them, mending nets, an "old-salt" friend
    of mine.
That old-salt friend of mine—how we love to talk together!
    Breathless is the wonder of his tales about the sea!
His face is tanned and wrinkled by the roughest kind of
  weather,
    And he is like a hero in a story-book to me!

Down among the wharves when a stiff north wind is
  flying,
    Schooners rub and bump against the docks they lie
    beside;
Half-way up the masts, the billowed sails are pulled for
  drying;
    Hawsers all are straining at the turning of the tide.
The turning of the tide! Time of wonder and of dreaming!
    Fishing-sloops are slipping from their docks across
    the way;
How our wharf reechoes when their saucy tugs are
  screaming!
    How the green piles whiten with the tossing of
    their spray!

Down among the wharves among a wonderland of
  shipping—
    Rows of shining, slender masts that sway against the sky!
Every day at flood of tide we watch some schooner slipping
    Out among the circling gulls, my old-salt friend and I.
My old salt-friend and I—he will drop the nets he's
  mending,

Watch with me each flapping jib, each straining yard
and spar;
How we thrill together when the sails are full and
bending—
We who like to wander where the waiting vessels are!

Eleanore Myers Jewett

OLD SHIP RIGGERS

Yes, we did a heap o' riggin'
In those rampin' boomin' days,
When the wooden ships were buildin'
On their quaint old greasy ways;
Crafts of every sort an' fashion,
Big an' little, lithe an' tall,
Had their birthplace by the harbor,
An' we rigged 'em one and all.

Jacob's ladder wasn't in it
With the riggin' on those ships
From the trunnels and the keelson
To the pointed royal tips;
That old ladder was for angels
Comin' down from up aloft,
With their wings an' gleamin' garments,
An' their hands all white an' soft.

Our riggin' was for sailors,
Tough an' hardy Bluenose dogs,
With their hands as hard as leather,
An' their boots thick heavy clogs,
They were nuthin' much like angels,
But they'd learned their business right,
An' they trusted to our riggin'
When the sea was roarin' white.

Seemed like fittin' out a maiden
For her happy weddin' day,
When we rigged a noble vessel,
Where she calm at anchor lay;
All her gear was new an' shiny,
Every ribbon taut an' trim,
An' she stood, when she was finished,
Tall an' handsome, straight an' slim.

When at last she slipped her moorin's,
An' slow-footed down the stream,
With her riggin' all aglowin',
An' her canvas all agleam,
How we cheered her to the echo,
An' our hearts thrilled high with pride,
As the ocean strode to meet her
For his own sea-royal bride.

Some came back just as they left us,
Trim an' spotless, buoyant, free;
Others crept up into harbor,
Scarred an' broken out at sea;
These we nursed like tender mothers,
Mendin' canvas, rope an' spar,
Till we had 'em all ashinin'
Like some twinklin' mornin' star.

But our riggin' days are over,
An' the past seems like a dream,
As we view the mighty changes
Brought about by wizard steam.
We are needed here no longer,
For there's nuthin' we can do—
Maybe there'll be work for riggers,
In the Port, beyond the blue.

H.A. Cody

THE SEAMAN'S LIFE

A Seaman's life is a life I love,
And one I'll live and die,
With the sea below and sky above,
    And the billows mountains high,
I love to hear the breakers dash
    And wild winds roar around,
The thunder roll and the lightning flash,
    And the sea birds' welcome sound.

Chorus
Then hurrah, for the deep, the briny deep,
    The boundless, glorious sea,
In a calm or storm in every form,
    A Seaman's life for me.

Some may boast of the grand and distant land,
    And the joys of a peaceful home,
I envy not their chosen lot,
    O give me the crested foam,
The gondolier in his bark may steer,
    O'er the rippling moonlight wave,
I laugh at his joys here's a toast to my boys,
    May the sea be our welcome grave.

When first I left my father's home,
    No joys it had for me
I long to lead a Sailor's life,
    Amidst the bold and free;
My heart was light and the sea was bright,
    When I joined the gallant crew,
The anchor weighed, and the sails unfurled.
    To my friends I bid adieu!

Sometimes when in the midnight watch,
    Upon the boundless sea,
In foreign climes I thought of her,
    Who a mother was to me,
I love her still and ever will,

When years perhaps are gone,
I shall return to my native shore,
  But the sea shall be my home.

I love to see the waves to dash,
  And to hear the boatswain's call,
'All hands reef topsails, be quick, my lads,
  For the storm is coming on;'
With the gallant crew up aloft I fly,
  While the sea is sparkling bright,
I am a merry laughing Sailor boy,
  And the sea is my delight.

Anonymous

EPITAPH FOR A SAILOR
BURIED ASHORE

He who but yesterday would roam
   Careless as clouds and currents range,
In homeless wandering most at home,
   Inhabiter of change;

Who wooed the West to win the East,
   And named the stars of North and South,
And felt the zest of Freedom's feast
   Familiar in his mouth;

Who found a faith in stranger-speech,
   And fellowship in foreign hands,
And had within his eager reach
   The relish of all lands—

How circumscribed a plot of earth
   Keeps now his restless footsteps still,
Whose wish was wide as ocean's girth,
   Whose will the water's will!

Charles G.D. Roberts

THE LOOKOUT

Low lies the land upon the sea.
Night speeds the sun into the west.
All's well, the course is set, our craft runs free.
The lookout's in his swaying nest.

Oh! humble man that you should stand
For magic hours at night, twixt sea and sky.
Alone with awe-struck gaze you scan
The blazing vaults where jewelled chariots fly.

Mark well Polaris, for its icy fire.
Take heart in their confiding leap
That beckoned men when Hiram sailed from Tyre.
Undimmed, they still a gleaming vigil keep.

You gaze, all enthroned atop the rugged spars.
Dim masthead lights, like jewelled fingers sway
In humble tribute to the flickering stars.
Sail on and watch, while day moves into day.

Now comes a sudden wind to break the spell.
A stir, like infants' voices calling from their sleep.
The stars invite, dream on, all's well.
'Twas but the hand of God upon the deep.

William Collins

DRINKING SONG

Fill, lads, fill;
  Fill, lads, fill.
Here we have a cure
  For every ill.
If fortune's unkind
As the north-east wind,
Still we must endure,
Trusting to our cure,
  In better luck still.

  Drink, boys, drink;
  Drink, boys, drink.
The bowl let us drain,
  With right good-will.
If women deceive
Why should we grieve?
Forgetting our pain,
Love make again,
  With better luck still.

  Sing, lads, sing;
  Sing, lads, sing.
Our voices we'll raise;
  Be merry still;
If dead to-morrow,
We brave all sorrow,
Life's a weary maze—
When we end our days,
  'Tis better luck still.

Frederick Marryat

THE MARINERS' COMPASS

Sam Spritsail's a lad you'd delight in,
For friendship, he's ever agog,
Loves his King, loves his wench, loves fighting,
And he loves, to be sure he does, GROG.
Says Sam, says he, life's all a notion,
And wants from the spirits a jog,
The world is a wide troubled ocean,
And our rudder and compass is GROG.

> *For grog is our larboard and starboard,*
> *Our Mainmast, our Mizen, our Log,*
> *At sea, or ashore, or when harboured,*
> *The Mariners' compass is grog.*

Let but GROG take its charge of the helm,
We perceive not the dangers of Sea,
Or if billows the vessel o'erwhelm,
Still GROG is the pilot for me.
Since GROG saves the trouble of thinking,
Then here's to each bold jolly dog,
For he that delights in good drinking,
Will toss off his full can of GROG.

> *For grog, etc.*

Sam Spritsail, though GROG he lov'd dearly,
And its praise he enraptur'd would sing,
Yet he fought for his country most cheerly,
Lov'd his sweetheart, honour'd his King.
For Sam's heart was splic'd to his Nancy's,
And his mind on the wench quite agog,
Yet Sailors have comical fancies,
And dear as his Nance, he loves GROG,

> *For grog, etc.*

Anonymous

NOTHING LIKE GROG

A plague of those musty old lubbers
   Who teach us to fast and to think,
And patient fall in with life's rubbers,
   With nothing but water to drink!
A can of good stuff, had they twigg'd it
   Would have set them for pleasure agog;
     And spite of the rules
     Of the schools, the old fools
Would all of 'em have swigg'd it,
   And swore there was nothing like grog!

My father, when last I from Guinea
   Return'd with abundance of wealth,
Cried, 'Jack, never be such a ninny
   To drink.' Says I, 'Father, your health!'
So I passed round the stuff—soon he twigg'd it,
   And it set the old codger agog;
     And he swigg'd, and mother,
     And sister and brother,
And I swigg'd, and all of us swigg'd it,
   And swore there was nothing like grog!

One day, when the chaplain was preaching,
   Behind him I curiously slunk;
And, while he our duty was teaching,
   As how we should never get drunk,
I tipp'd him the stuff, and he twigg'd it,
   Which soon set his rev'rence agog,
     And he swigg'd, and Nick swigg'd,
     And Ben swigg'd, and Dick swigg'd,
And I swigg'd and all of us swigg'd it,
   And swore there was nothing like grog!

Then trust me, there's nothing as drinking
   So pleasant on this side the grave.
It keeps the unhappy from thinking,
   And makes e'en the valiant more brave.
For me, from the moment I twigg'd it.
   The good stuff has so set me agog,
     Sick or well, late or early,
     Wind foully or fairly,
I've constantly swigg'd it,
   And, damme! there's nothing like grog.

Charles Dibdin

SAM SWIPES

Sam Swipes, he was a seaman true,
   As brave and bold a tar
As e'er was dressed in navy blue
   On board a man-of-war.

One fault he had—on sea or land
   He was a thirsty dog;
For Sammy never could withstand
   A glass or so of grog.

He always like to be at sea,
   For e'en on shore, the rover,
If not as drunk as he could be,
   Was always 'half seas over.'

The gunner, who was apt to scoff
   With jokes most aptly timed,
Said Sam might any day go off,
   'Cause he was always 'primed.'

Sam didn't want a feeling heart,
   Though never seen to cry;
Yet tears were always on the start,
   'The drop was in his eye.'

At fighting Sam was never shy,
   A most undoubted merit;
His courage never failed, and why?
   He was so full of 'spirit.'

In action he had lost an eye,
   But that gave him no trouble;
Quoth Sam, 'I have no cause to sigh,
   I'm always "seeing double." '

A shot from an unlucky gun
   Put Sam on timber pegs;
It didn't signify to one
   Who ne'er could 'keep his legs.'

One night he filled a pail with grog,
  Determined he would suck it;
He drained it dry, the thirsty dog!
  Hiccupped, and 'kicked the bucket.'

Frederick Marryat

RIVETS

My grandfather's hands were wise and hard
For he swung his adze in a Salem yard
And thumbed his planks and drove his nails
Till he learned his trade from strake to rails
And could dream a ship till he saw her whole
With royals set, and feel her roll
And lift her bows like a dripping blade
In the spacious swells of the India Trade.
...He's long been dead, and his ships are junk,
All rotting askew, or stripped or sunk.
But when they were loosed and took their slide
And squared away on the greasy tide,
He hitched up his belt, and "By God," said he,
"No sweeter ship has sailed the sea;
And she's all mine, yes, every inch,
From the spring of her heel to the swell of her winch!"
And he dusted his hands and wiped his face
And stood up his sledge in its proper place.
...And I swing here on a plank in a bight
Catching hot rivets from morning till night.
They've never told me who planned the craft
Or where they'll route the riveted raft:
Perhaps she'll do a tourist turn
And pack high hats with money to burn,
Or carry cargo of frozen meat
For Argentine, or hides or wheat.
They don't tell me; but I hear the clang
Of the hammers going, and see the gang
Ahoisting beams like a skyscraper frame
And bolting them in, and always the same
And all day long. I do my stunt
Of rackety rack and buntity bunt.
It's got to be so, for it's part of the plan
But I wonder some if I'm really a man.
...She'll soon be done and I'll be through.
They'll give me my time when my time is due.

I s'pose I've done my share of the trick,
They treat me right, and I shouldn't kick.
So I'll shed my jeans and I'll count my pay
And call it the end of a perfect day.
But all I'll own of the old man's pride
Are rows of rivets along her side.

N.S. Olds

THE TIDE RISES, THE TIDE FALLS

The tide rises, the tide falls,
The twilight darkens, the curlew calls;
   Along the sea-sands damp and brown
   The traveller hastens toward the town,
And the tide rises, the tide falls.

Darkness settles on roofs and walls,
But the sea, the sea in the darkness calls;
   The little waves, with their soft, white hands,
   Efface the footprints in the sands,
And the tide rises, the tide falls.

The morning breaks; the steeds in their stalls
Stamp and neigh, as the hostler calls;
   The day returns, but nevermore
   Returns the traveller to the shore,
And the tide rises, the tide falls.

Henry Wadsworth Longfellow

SAILOR MAN

He was one who followed
Dreams and stars and ships,
They say the wind had fastened
Strange words upon his lips.

There was something secret
In the way he smiled
As if he could remember
The laughter of a child.

Wayward as a seagull,
Lonely as a hawk
Yet he believed in fairies
And heard the mermaids talk.

Nothing ever held him
Longer than a day,
They speak of him as careless,
And whimsical and gay;

But I think he swaggered
So he could pretend
The other side of Nowhere
Led somewhere in the end.

H. Sewell Bailey

LOW-TIDE

These wet rocks where the tide has been,
  Barnacled white and weeded brown
And slimed beneath to a beautiful green,
  These wet rocks where the tide went down
Will show again when the tide is high
  Faint and perilous, far from shore,
No place to dream, but a place to die,—
  The bottom of the sea once more.
There was a child that wandered through
  A giant's empty house all day.—
House full of wonderful things and new,
  But no fit place for a child to play.

Edna St. Vincent Millay

WHERE LIES THE LAND?

Where lies the land to which the ship would go?
Far, far ahead, is all her seamen know.
And where the land she travels from? Away,
Far, far behind, is all that they can say.

On sunny noons upon the deck's smooth face,
Linked arm in arm, how pleasant here to pace;
Or, o'er the stern reclining, watch below
The foaming wake far widening as we go.

On stormy nights when wild northwesters rave,
How proud a thing to fight with wind and wave!
The dripping sailor on the reeling mast
Exults to bear, and scorns to wish it past.

Where lies the land to which the ship would go?
Far, far ahead, is all her seamen know.
And where the land she travels from? Away,
Far, far behind, is all that they can say.

Arthur Hugh Clough

THE RIME OF THE ANCIENT MARINER
IN SEVEN PARTS

ARGUMENT.—How a Ship having passed the Line was driven by storms to the cold Country towards the South Pole; and how from thence she made her course to the tropical Latitude of the Great Pacific Ocean; and of the strange things that befell; and in what manner the Ancyent Marinere came back to his own Country.

PART I

It is an ancient Mariner,
And he stoppeth one of three.
"By thy long grey beard and glittering eye,
Now wherefore stopp'st thou me?

An ancient Mariner meeteth three Gallants bidden to a wedding-feast, and detaineth one

"The Bridegroom's doors are opened wide,
And I am next of kin;
The guests are met, the feast is set:
May'st hear the merry din."

He holds him with his skinny hand,
"There was a ship," quoth he.
"Hold off! unhand me, grey-beard loon!"
Eftsoons his hand dropt he.

He holds him with his glittering eye—
The Wedding-Guest stood still,
And listens like a three years' child:
The Mariner hath his will.

The Wedding-Guest is spellbound by the eye of the old seafaring man, and constrained to hear his tale

The Wedding-Guest sat on a stone:
He cannot choose but hear;
And thus spake on that ancient man,
The bright-eyed Mariner.

"The ship was cheered, the harbour cleared,
Merrily did we drop
Below the kirk, below the hill,
Below the lighthouse top.

"The sun came up upon the left,
Out of the sea came he!
And he shone bright, and on the right
Went down into the sea.

The Mariner tells how the ship sailed southward with a good wind and fair weather, till it reached the line

75

"Higher and higher every day,
Till over the mast at noon—"
The Wedding-Guest here beat his breast,
For he heard the loud bassoon.

The
Wedding-Guest
heareth the
bridal music;
but the Mariner
continueth his
tale

The bride hath paced into the hall,
Red as a rose is she;
Nodding their heads before her goes
The merry minstrelsy.

The Wedding-Guest he beat his breast,
Yet he cannot choose but hear;
And thus spake on that ancient man,
The bright-eyed Mariner.

The ship
driven by a
storm toward
the south pole

"And now the Storm-blast came, and he
Was tyrannous and strong:
He struck with his o'ertaking wings,
And chased us south along.

"With sloping masts and dipping prow,
As who pursued with yell and blow
Still treads the shadow of his foe,
And forward bends his head,
The ship drove fast, loud roared the blast,
And southward aye we fled.

"And now there came both mist and snow,
And it grew wondrous cold:
And ice, mast-high, came floating by,
As green as emerald.

The land of ice,
and of fearful
sounds where
no living thing
was to be seen

"And through the drifts the snowy clifts
Did send a dismal sheen:
Nor shapes of men nor beasts we ken—
The ice was all between.

"The ice was here, the ice was there,
The ice was all around:
It cracked and growled, and roared and howled,
Like noises in a swound!

"At length did cross an Albatross,
Thorough the fog it came;
As if it had been a Christian soul,
We hailed it in God's name.

"It ate the food it ne'er had eat,
And round and round it flew.
The ice did split with a thunder-fit;
The helmsman steered us through!

"And a good south wind sprung up behind;
The Albatross did follow,
And every day, for food or play,
Came to the mariners' hollo!

"In mist or cloud, on mast or shroud,
It perched for vespers nine;
Whiles all the night, through fog-smoke white,
Glimmered the white moon-shine."

"God save thee, ancient Mariner!
From the fiends,that plague thee thus!—
Why look'st thou so?"—With my cross-bow
I shot the Albatross.

PART II

The Sun now rose upon the right:
Out of the sea came he,
Still hid in mist, and on the left
Went down into the sea.

And the good south wind still blew behind,
But no sweet bird did follow,
Nor any day for food or play
Came to the mariners' hollo!

And I had done a hellish thing,
And it would work 'em woe:
For all averred, I had killed the bird
That made the breeze to blow.
Ah wretch! said they, the bird to slay,
That made the breeze to blow!

Till a great sea-bird, called the Albatross, came through the snow-fog, and was received with great joy and hospitality

And lo! the Albatross proveth a bird of good omen, and followeth the ship as it returned northward through fog and floating ice

The ancient Mariner inhospitably killeth the pious bird of good omen

His shipmates cry out against the ancient Mariner, for killing the bird of good luck

But when the
fog cleared off,
they justify the
same, and thus
make
themselves
accomplices in
the crime

Nor dim nor red, like God's own head,
The glorious Sun uprist:
Then all averred, I had killed the bird
That brought the fog and mist.
'Twas right, said they, such birds to slay,
That bring the fog and mist.

The fair breeze
continues; the
ship enters the
Pacific Ocean,
and sails
northward,
even till it
reaches the
Line

The fair breeze blew, the white foam flew,
The furrow followed free;
We were the first that ever burst
Into that silent sea.

The ship hath
been suddenly
becalmed

Down dropt the breeze, the sails dropt down,
'Twas sad as sad could be;
And we did speak only to break
The silence of the sea!

All in a hot and copper sky,
The bloody Sun, at noon,
Right up above the mast did stand,
No bigger than the Moon.

Day after day, day after day,
We stuck, nor breath nor motion;
As idle as a painted ship
Upon a painted ocean.

And the
Albatross
begins to be
avenged

Water, water, every where,
And all the boards did shrink;
Water, water, every where
Nor any drop to drink.

The very deep did rot: O Christ!
That ever this should be!
Yea, slimy things did crawl with legs
Upon the slimy sea.

About, about, in reel and rout
The death-fires danced at night;
The water, like a witch's oils,
Burnt green, and blue and white.

And some in dreams assured were
Of the Spirit that plagued us so,
Nine fathom deep he had followed us
From the land of mist and snow.

And every tongue, through utter drought,
Was withered at the root;
We could not speak, no more than if
We had been choked with soot.

Ah! well a-day! what evil looks
Had I from old and young!
Instead of the cross, the Albatross
About my neck was hung.

PART III

There passed a weary time. Each throat
Was parched, and glazed each eye.
A weary time! a weary time!
How glazed each weary eye,
When looking westward, I beheld
A something in the sky.

At first it seemed a little speck,
And then it seemed a mist;
It moved and moved, and took at last
A certain shape, I wist.

A speck, a mist, a shape, I wist!
And still it neared and neared:
As if it dodged a water-sprite,
It plunged and tacked and veered.

A Spirit had followed them; one of the invisible inhabitants of this planet, neither departed souls nor angels: concerning whom the learned Jew, Josephus, and the Platonic Constantino-politan, Michael Psellus, may be consulted. They are very numerous, and there is no climate or element without one or more

The shipmates, in their sore distress, would fain throw the whole guilt on the ancient Mariner: in sign whereof they hang the dead sea-bird round his neck

The ancient Mariner beholdeth a sign in the element afar off

With throats unslaked, with black lips baked,
We could nor laugh nor wail;
Through utter drought all dumb we stood!
I bit my arm, I sucked the blood,
And cried, A sail! a sail!

With throats unslaked, with black lips baked,
Agape they heard me call:
Gramercy! they for joy did grin,
And all at once their breath drew in,
As they were drinking all.

See! see! (I cried) she tacks no more!
Hither to work us weal;
Without a breeze, without a tide,
She steadies with upright keel!

The western wave was all a-flame.
The day was well nigh done!
Almost upon the western wave
Rested the broad bright Sun;
When that strange shape drove suddenly
Betwixt us and the Sun.

And straight the Sun was flecked with bars,
(Heaven's Mother send us grace!)
As if through a dungeon-grate he peered
With broad and burning face.

Alas! (thought I, and my heard beat loud)
How fast she nears and nears!
Are those her sails that glance in the Sun,
Like restless gossameres?

Are those her ribs through which the Sun
Did peer, as through a grate?
And is that Woman all her crew?
Is that a Death? and are there two?
Is Death that woman's mate?

Her lips were red, her looks were free,
Her locks were yellow as gold:
Her skin was as white as leprosy,

At its nearer approach, it seemeth him to be a ship; and at a dear ransom he freeth his speech from the bonds of thirst

A flash of joy;

And horror follows. For can it be a ship that comes onward without wind or tide?

It seemeth him but the skeleton of a ship

And its ribs are seen as bars on the face of the setting Sun. The Spectre-Woman and her Deathmate, and no other on board the skelton-ship

The Night-mare Life-in-Death was she,
Who thicks man's blood with cold.

Like vessel,
like crew!

The naked hulk alongside came,
And the twain were casting dice;
"The game is done! I've won! I've won!"
Quoth she, and whistles thrice.

Death and
Life-in-Death
have diced for
the ship's
crew, and she
(the latter)
winneth the
ancient
Mariner

The Sun's rim dips; the stars rush out:
At one stride comes the dark;
With far-heard whisper, o'er the sea,
Off shot the spectre-bark.

No twilight
within the
courts of the
sun

We listened and looked sideways up!
Fear at my heart, as at a cup,
My life-blood seemed to sip!
The stars were dim, and thick the night,
The steerman's face by his lamp gleamed white;
From the sails the dew did drip—
Till clomb above the eastern bar
The horned Moon, with one bright star
Within the nether tip.

At the rising of
the Moon,

One after one, by the star-dogged Moon,
Too quick for groan or sigh,
Each turned his face with a ghastly pang,
And cursed me with his eye.

One after
another,

Four times fifty living men,
(And I heard nor sigh nor groan)
With heavy thump, a lifeless lump,
They dropped down one by one.

His shipmates
drop down
dead

The souls did from their bodies fly,—
They fled to bliss or woe!
And every soul, it passed me by,
Like the whizz of my cross-bow!

But
Life-in-Death
begins her
work on the
ancient
Mariner

PART IV

The
Wedding-
Guest
feareth that a
Spirit is talking
to him;

"I fear thee, ancient Mariner!
I fear thy skinny hand!
And thou art long, and lank, and brown,
As is the ribbed sea-sand.

But the ancient
Mariner
assureth him of
his bodily life,
and
proceedeth to
relate his
horrible
penance

"I fear thee and thy glittering eye,
And thy skinny hand, so brown."—
Fear not, fear not, thou Wedding-Guest!
This body dropt not down.

Alone, alone, all, all alone,
Alone on a wide wide sea!
And never a saint took pity on
My soul in agony.

He despiseth
the creatures of
the calm

The many men, so beautiful!
And they all dead did lie:
And a thousand thousand slimy things
Lived on; and so did I.

And envieth
that they
should live,
and so many lie
dead

I looked upon the rotting sea,
And drew my eyes away;
I looked upon the rotting deck,
And there the dead men lay.

I looked to heaven, and tried to pray;
But or ever a prayer had gusht,
A wicked whisper came, and made
My heart as dry as dust.

I closed my lids, and kept them close,
And the balls like pulses beat;
For the sky and the sea, and the sea and the sky
Lay like a load on my weary eye,
And the dead were at my feet.

But the curse
liveth for him
in the eye of the
dead men

The cold sweat melted from their limbs,
Nor rot nor reek did they:
The look with which they looked on me
Had never passed away.

An orphan's curse would drag to hell
A spirit from on high;
But oh! more horrible than that
Is the curse in a dead man's eye!
Seven days, seven nights, I saw that curse,
And yet I could not die.

The moving Moon went up the sky,
And no where did abide:
Softly she was going up,
And a star or two beside—

Her beams bemocked the sultry main,
Like April hoar-frost spread;
But where the ship's huge shadow lay,
The charmed water burnt alway
A still and awful red.

Beyond the shadow of the ship,
I watched the water-snakes:
They moved in tracks of shining white,
And when they reared, the elfish light
Fell off in hoary flakes.

Within the shadow of the ship
I watched their rich attire:
Blue, glossy green, and velvet black,
They coiled and swam; and every track
Was a flash of golden fire.

O happy living things! no tongue
Their beauty might declare:
A spring of love gushed from my heart,
And I blessed them unaware:
Sure my kind saint took pity on me,
And I blessed them unaware.

The selfsame moment I could pray;
And from my neck so free
The Albatross fell off, and sank
Like lead into the sea.

In his loneliness and fixedness he yearneth towards the journeying Moon, and the stars that still sojourn, yet still move onward; and everywhere the blue sky belongs to them, and is their appointed rest, and their native country and their own natural homes, which they enter unannounced, as lords that are certainly expected and yet there is a silent joy at their arrival

By the light of the Moon he beholdeth God's creatures of the great calm

Their beauty and their happiness

He blesseth them in his heart

The spell begins to break

PART V

Oh sleep! it is a gentle thing,
Beloved from pole to pole!
To Mary Queen the praise be given!
She sent the gentle sleep from Heaven,
That slid into my soul.

The silly buckets on the deck,
That had so long remained,
I dreamt that they were filled with dew;
And when I awoke, it rained.

My lips were wet, my throat was cold,
My garments all were dank;
Sure I had drunken in my dreams,
And still my body drank.

I moved, and could not feel my limbs:
I was so light—almost
I thought that I had died in sleep,
And was a blessed ghost.

And soon I heard a roaring wind:
It did not come anear;
But with its sounds it shook the sails,
That were so thin and sere.

The upper air burst into life!
And a hundred fire-flags sheen,
To and fro they were hurried about!
And to and fro, and in and out,
The wan stars danced between.

And the coming wind did roar more loud,
And the sails did sigh like sedge;
And the rain poured down from one black cloud;
The Moon was at its edge.

The thick black cloud was cleft, and still
The Moon was at its side:
Like waters shot from some high crag,
The lightning fell with never a jag,
A river steep and wide.

The loud wind never reached the ship,
Yet now the ship moved on!
Beneath the lightning and the Moon
The dead men gave a groan.

The bodies of
the ship's crew
are inspired,
and the ship
moves on;

They groaned, they stirred, they all uprose,
Nor spake, nor moved their eyes;
It had been strange, even in a dream,
To have seen those dead men rise.

The helmsman steered, the ship moved on;
Yet never a breeze up blew;
The mariners all 'gan work the ropes,
Where they were wont to do;
They raised their limbs like lifeless tools—
We were a ghastly crew.

The body of my brother's son
Stood by me, knee to knee:
The body and I pulled at one rope
But he said nought to me.

But not by the
souls of the
men, nor by
daemons of
earth or middle
air, but by a
blessed troop
of angelic
spirits, sent
down by the
invocation of
the guardian
saint

"I fear thee, ancient Mariner!"
Be calm, thou Wedding-Guest!
'Twas not those souls that fled in pain,
Which to their corses came again,
But a troop of spirits blest:

For when it dawned—they dropped their arms,
And clustered round the mast;
Sweet sounds rose slowly through their mouths,
And from their bodies passed.

Around, around, flew each sweet sound,
Then darted to the Sun;
Slowly the sounds came back again,
Now mixed, now one by one.

Sometimes a-dropping from the sky
I heard the sky-lark sing;
Sometimes all little birds that are,
How they seemed to fill the sea and air
With their sweet jargoning!

And now 'twas like all instruments,
Now like a lonely flute;
And now it is an angel's song,
That makes the heavens be mute.

It ceased; yet still the sails made on
A pleasant noise till noon,
A noise like of a hidden brook
In the leafy month of June,
That to the sleeping woods all night
Singeth a quiet tune.

Till noon we quietly sailed on,
Yet never a breeze did breathe:
Slowly and smoothly went the ship,
Moved onward from beneath.

Under the keel nine fathom deep,
From the land of mist and snow,
The spirit slid: and it was he
That made the ship to go.
The sails at noon left off their tune,
And the ship stood still also.

The Sun, right up above the mast,
Had fixed her to the ocean:
But in a minute she 'gan stir,
With a short uneasy motion—
Backwards and forwards half her length
With a short uneasy motion.

Then like a pawing horse let go,
She made a sudden bound:
It flung the blood into my head,
And I fell down in a swound.

How long in that same fit I lay,
I have not to declare;
But ere my living life returned,
I heard and in my soul discerned
Two voices in the air.

"Is it he?" quoth one, "Is this the man?
By him who died on cross,
With his cruel bow he laid full low
The harmless Albatross.

"The spirit who bideth by himself
In the land of mist and snow,
He loved the bird that loved the man
Who shot him with his bow."

The other was a softer voice,
As soft as honey-dew:
Quoth he, "The man hath penance done,
And penance more will do."

PART VI

FIRST VOICE

"But tell me, tell me! speak again,
Thy soft response renewing—
What makes that ship drive on so fast?
What is the ocean doing?"

SECOND VOICE

"Still as a slave before his lord,
The ocean hath no blast;
His great bright eye most silently
Up to the moon is cast—

"If he may know which way to go;
For she guides him smooth or grim.
See, brother, see! how graciously
She looketh down on him."

FIRST VOICE

"But why drives on that ship so fast,
Without or wave or wind?"

two of them relate, one to the other, that penance long and heavy for the ancient Mariner hath been accorded to the Polar Spirit, who returneth southward

The Mariner hath been cast into a trance; for the angelic power causeth the vessel to

SECOND VOICE

"The air is cut away before,
And closes from behind.
"Fly, brother, fly! more high, more high!
Or we shall be belated.
For slow and slow that ship will go,
When the Mariner's trance is abated."

drive
northward
faster than
human life
could endure

I woke, and we were sailing on
As in a gentle weather:
'Twas night, calm night, the moon was high,
The dead men stood together.

The
supernatural
motion is
retarded; the
Mariner
awakes, and
his penance
begins anew

All stood together on the deck,
For a charnel-dungeon fitter:
All fixed on me their stony eyes,
That in the Moon did glitter.

The pang, the curse, with which they died,
Had never passed away:
I could not draw my eyes from theirs,
Nor turn them up to pray.

The curse is
finally expiated

And now this spell was snapt: once more
I viewed the ocean green,
And looked far forth, yet little saw
Of what had else been seen—

Like one, that on a lonesome road
Doth walk in fear and dread,
And having once turned round walks on,
And turns no more his head;
Because he knows, a frightful fiend
Doth close behind him tread.

But soon there breathed a wind on me,
Nor sound nor motion made:
Its path was not upon the sea,
In ripple or in shade.

It raised my hair, it fanned my cheek
Like a meadow-gale of spring—
It mingled strangely with my fears,
Yet it felt like a welcoming.

Swiftly, swiftly flew the ship,
Yet she sailed softly too:
Sweetly, sweetly blew the breeze—
On me alone it blew.

Oh! dream of joy! is this indeed
The light-house top I see?
Is this the hill? is this the kirk?
Is this mine own countree?

We drifted o'er the harbour-bar,
And I with sobs did pray—
O let me be awake, my God!
Or let me sleep alway.

The harbour-bay was clear as glass,
So smoothly it was strewn!
And on the bay the moonlight lay,
And the shadow of the Moon.

The rock shone bright, the kirk no less,
That stands above the rock:
The moonlight steeped in silentness
The steady weathercock.

And the bay was white with silent light
Till rising from the same,
Full many shapes, that shadows were,
In crimson colours came.

A little distance from the prow
Those crimson shadows were:
I turned my eyes upon the deck—
Oh, Christ! what saw I there!

Each corse lay flat, lifeless and flat.
And, by the holy rood!
A man all light, a seraph-man,
On every corse there stood.

And the Ancient Mariner beholdeth his native country

The Angelic spirits leave the dead bodies,

And appear in their own forms of light

89

This seraph-band, each waved his hand:
It was a heavenly sight!
They stood as signals to the land,
Each one a lovely light;

This seraph-band, each waved his hand,
No voice did they impart—
No voice; but oh! the silence sank
Like music on my heart.

But soon I heard the dash of oars,
I heard the Pilot's cheer;
My head was turned perforce away,
And I saw a boat appear.

The Pilot and the Pilot's boy,
I heard them coming fast:
Dear Lord in Heaven! it was a joy
The dead men could not blast.

I saw a third—I heard his voice:
It is the Hermit good!
He singeth loud his godly hymns
That he makes in the wood.
He'll shrieve my soul, he'll wash away
The Albatross's blood.

PART VII

The Hermit of
the Wood

This Hermit good lives in that wood
Which slopes down to the sea.
How loudly his sweet voice he rears!
He loves to talk with marineres
That come from a far countree.

He kneels at morn, and noon, and eve—
He hath a cushion plump:
It is the moss that wholly hides
The rotted old oak-stump.

The skiff-boat neared: I heard them talk,
"Why, this is strange, I trow!
Where are those lights so many and fair,
That signal made but now?"

"Strange, by my faith!" the Hermit said—
"And they answered not our cheer!
The planks looked warped! and see those sails,
How thin they are and sere!
I never saw aught like to them,
Unless perchance it were

Approacheth
the ship with
wonder

"Brown skeletons of leaves that lag
My forest-brook along;
When the ivy-tod is heavy with snow,
And the owlet whoops to the wolf below,
That eats the she-wolf's young."

"Dear Lord! it hath a fiendish look—
(The Pilot made reply)
I am a-feared"—"Push on, push on!"
Said the Hermit cheerily.

The boat came closer to the ship,
But I nor spake nor stirred;
The boat came close beneath the ship,
And straight a sound was heard.

Under the water it rumbled on,
Still louder and more dread:
It reached the ship, it split the bay;
The ship went down like lead.

The ship
suddenly
sinketh

Stunned by that loud and dreadful sound,
Which sky and ocean smote,
Like one that hath been seven days drowned
My body lay afloat;
But swift as dreams, myself I found
Within the Pilot's boat.

The ancient
Mariner is
saved in the
Pilot's boat

Upon the whirl, where sank the ship,
The boat spun round and round;
And all was still, save that the hill
Was telling of the sound.

I moved my lips—the Pilot shrieked
And fell down in a fit;
The holy Hermit raised his eyes,
And prayed where he did sit.

I took the oars: the Pilot's boy,
Who now doth crazy go,
Laughed loud and long, and all the while
His eyes went to and fro.
"Ha! ha!" quoth he, "full plain I see,
The Devil knows how to row."

And now, all in my own countree,
I stood on the firm land!
The Hermit stepped forth from the boat,
And scarcely he could stand.

"O shrieve me, shrieve me, holy man!"
The Hermit crossed his brow.
"Say quick," quoth he, "I bid thee say—
What manner of man art thou?"

The ancient
Mariner
earnestly
entreateth the
Hermit to
shrieve him;
and the
penance of life
falls on him

Forthwith this frame of mine was wrenched
With a woful agony,
Which forced me to begin my tale;
And then it left me free.

And ever and
anon
throughout his
future life an
agony
constraineth
him to travel
from land to
land,

Since then, at an uncertain hour,
That agony returns:
And till my ghastly tale is told,
This heart within me burns.

I pass, like night, from land to land;
I have strange power of speech;
That moment that his face I see,
I know the man that must hear me:
To him my tale I teach.

What loud uproar bursts from that door!
The wedding-guests are there:
But in the garden-bower the bride
And bride-maids singing are:
And hark the little vesper bell
Which biddeth me to prayer!

O Wedding-Guest! this soul hath been
Alone on a wide wide sea:
So lonely 'twas, that God himself
Scarce seemed there to be.

O sweeter than the marriage-feast,
'Tis sweeter far to me,
To walk together to the kirk
With a goodly company!—

To walk together to the kirk,
And all together pray,
While each to his great Father bends,
Old men, and babes, and loving friends
And youths and maidens gay!

Farewell, farewell! but this I tell
To thee, thou Wedding-Guest!
He prayeth well, who loveth well
Both man and bird and beast.

And to teach,
by his own
example, love
and reverence
to all things
that God made
and loveth

He prayeth best, who loveth best
All things both great and small;
For the dear God who loveth us,
He made and loveth all.

The Mariner, whose eye is bright,
Whose beard with age is hoar,
Is gone: and now the Wedding-Guest
Turned from the bridegroom's door.

He went like one that hath been stunned,
And is of sense forlorn:
A sadder and a wiser man,
He rose the morrow morn.

Samuel Taylor Coleridge

HELL'S PAVEMENT

'When I'm discharged in Liverpool 'n' draws my bit o' pay,
   I won't come to sea no more.
I'll court a pretty little lass 'n' have a weddin' day,
   'N' settle somewhere down ashore.
I'll never fare to sea again a-temptin' Davy Jones,
A-hearkening to the cruel sharks a-hungerin' for my bones;
I'll run a blushin' dairy-farm or go a-crackin' stones,
   Or buy 'n' keep a little liquor-store,'—
              So he said.

They towed her in to Liverpool, we made the hooker fast,
   And the copper-bound officials paid the crew,
And Billy drew his money, but the money didn't last,
   For he painted the alongshore blue,—
It was rum for Poll, and rum for Nan, and gin for Jolly Jack.
He shipped a week later in the clothes upon his back,
He had to pinch a little straw, he had to beg a sack
   To sleep on, when his watch was through,—
              So he did.

John Masefield

CLEANING SHIP

Down on your knees, boys, holystone the decks,
Rub 'em down, scrub 'em down, stiffen out your necks,
For we're gettin' near t' home, lads, gettin' near t' home,
With a good stiff breeze and a wake o' shining foam.
Up on th' masts, boys, scrape 'em white an' clean,
Tar th' ropes an' paint th' rails an' stripe her sides with
   green,
For we're gettin' near t' home, lads, gettin' near t' home,
With a good stiff breeze an' a wake o' shining foam.

Charles Keeler

SEA CALL

My old love for the water has come back again—
  I had forgotten its surging, so long, so long away;
Sapphire-blue in the sunlight and green-gray in the rain,
  And the same waves cresting, and the same sharp spray;

There was left a wave in my heart when I went to the
  inland towns,
    Something that moved and murmured in the days
    when I forgot;
Vivid flowers of the gardens or thick long grass of the
  downs—
    What were the sweets of the summer days, where the
    calling waves were not?

My old love for the water has come back once more;
  The wave of the deep draws full, and the wave in my
  heart lifts high;
This is my own old country and my own old shore. . .
  And I cannot leave the water till the day I die.

                              Margaret Widdemer

BALLAD OF THE TEMPEST

We were crowded in the cabin,
Not a soul would dare to sleep,—
It was midnight on the waters,
And a storm was on the deep.

'T is a fearful thing in winter
To be shattered in the blast,
And to hear the rattling trumpet
Thunder, "Cut away the mast!"

So we shuddered there in silence,—
For the stoutest held his breath,
While the hungry sea was roaring,
And the breakers talked with Death.

As thus we sat in darkness,
Each one busy in his prayers,—
"We are lost!" the captain shouted,
As he staggered down the stairs.

But his little daughter whispered,
As she took his icy hand,
"Isn't God upon the ocean,
Just the same as on the land?"

Then we kissed the little maiden,
And we spoke in better cheer,
And we anchored safe in harbor
When the morn was shining clear.

James T. Fields

BEAUTIFUL PROUD SEA

Careless forever, beautiful proud sea,
  You laugh in happy thunder all alone,
You fold upon yourself, you dance your dance
  Impartially on drift-weed, sand or stone.
You make us believe that we can outlive death,
  You make us, for an instant, for your sake,
Burn, like stretched silver of a wave,
  Not breaking, but about to break.

Sara Teasdale

THE WRECK OF THE HESPERUS

It was the schooner *Hesperus,*
    That sailed the wintry sea;
And the skipper had taken his little daughter,
    To bear him company.

Blue were her eyes as the fairy-flax,
    Her cheeks like the dawn of day,
And her bosom white as the hawthorn buds,
    That ope in the month of May.

The skipper he stood beside the helm,
    His pipe was in his mouth,
And he watched how the veering flaw did blow
    The smoke now West, now South.

Then up and spake an old Sailor,
    Had sailed to the Spanish Main,
"I pray thee, put into yonder port,
    For I fear a hurricane.

"Last night, the moon had a golden ring,
    And tonight no moon we see!"
The skipper, he blew a whiff from his pipe,
    And a scornful laugh laughed he.

Colder and louder blew the wind,
    A gale from the Northeast,
The snow fell hissing in the brine,
    And the billows frothed like yeast.

Down came the storm, and smote amain
    The vessel in its strength;
She shuddered and paused, like a frightened steed,
    Then leaped her cable's length.

"Come hither! come hither! my little daughter,
    And do not tremble so;
For I can weather the roughest gale
    That ever wind did blow."

He wrapped her warm in his seaman's coat
  Against the stinging blast;
He cut a rope from a broken spar,
  And bound her to the mast.

"O father! I hear the church-bells ring,
  O say, what may it be?"
" 'T is a fog-bell on a rock-bound coast!"—
  And he steered for the open sea.

"O father! I hear the sound of guns,
  O say, what may it be?"
"Some ship in distress, that cannot live
  In such an angry sea!"

"O father! I see a gleaming light,
  O say, what may it be?"
But the father answered never a word,
  A frozen corpse was he.

Lashed to the helm, all stiff and stark,
  With his face turned to the skies,
The lantern gleamed through the gleaming snow
  On his fixed and glassy eyes.

Then the maiden clasped her hands and prayed
  That saved she might be;
And she thought of Christ, who stilled the wave,
  On the Lake of Galilee.

And fast through the midnight dark and drear
  Through the whistling sleet and snow,
Like a sheeted ghost, the vessel swept
  Tow'rds the Reef of Norman's Woe.

And ever the fitful gusts between
  A sound came from the land;
It was the sound of the trampling surf
  On the rocks and the hard sea-sand.

The breakers were right beneath her bows,
    She drifted a dreary wreck,
And a whooping billow swept the crew
    Like icicles from her deck.

She struck where the white and fleecy waves
    Looked soft as carded wool,
But the cruel rocks, they gored her side
    Like the horns of an angry bull.

Her rattling shrouds, all sheathed in ice,
    With the masts went by the board;
Like a vessel of glass, she stove and sank,
    Ho! ho! the breakers roared!

At daybreak, on the bleak sea-beach,
    A fisherman stood aghast,
To see the form of a maiden fair,
    Lashed close to a drifting mast.

The salt sea was frozen on her breast,
    The salt tears in her eyes;
And he saw her hair, like the brown sea-weed,
    On the billows fall and rise.

Such was the wreck of the *Hesperus*,
    In the midnight and the snow!
Christ save us all from a death like this,
    On the reef of Norman's Woe!

Henry Wadsworth Longfellow

TIDES

I

Here to the sweep of the shore
The changeful waters come—
Now ruthless in uproar,
Now crooningly, now dumb.

To-day on a dawn of spring
They sang at their silver loom,
To-morrow the trembling shore will ring
With pitiless strokes of doom.

What is this ebb and flow—
This ceaseless swing of the sea,
This sounding to and fro
On earth's great organ-key?

Ask of the ships that ride
Or the passionate winds that sweep,
But the laws of the rhythmic tide
Are not for them to keep.

Immutably bound, yet free,
Constant as moon or sun,
Moving to some divine decree,
The world's great waters run.

II

And we that watch and wait
Breathing with mortal breath,
We are but ships upon that sea
Whose tides are birth and death.

Sailing out of the dark,
O little ships, to the light,
And never too small or frail a bark
To sail to the Infinite!

But what of the storms that hide
In that rhythmic mystery?
And what of the bitter, ultimate tide
We neither hear nor see?

Be still, O querulous soul!
He hath charted every sea,
And the Master of all the tides that roll
Shall send to pilot thee.

A.G. Prys-Jones

ONCE BY THE PACIFIC

The shattered water made a misty din.
Great waves looked over others coming in.
And thought of doing something to the shore
That water never did to land before.
The clouds were low and hairy in the skies,
Like locks blown forward in the gleam of eyes.
You could not tell, and yet it looked as if
The shore was lucky in being backed by cliff,
The cliff in being backed by continent;
It looked as if a night of dark intent
Was coming, and not only a night, an age.
Someone had better be prepared for rage.
There would be more than ocean-water broken
Before God's last *Put out the Light* was spoken.

Robert Frost

TO THE HUMPBACK WHALES

Come you baleened behemoths
You large brained beauties
Share what's on your minds
You spent several million years
Swimming around with few enemies
Until a killer species appeared
You had sufficient time to think
To compose symphonies, to meditate
About the creator of cetacean kind.
We once had a philosopher named Thales
Who maintained that all things are water
Thales! Whales! Do you read me?

Look, you large lunged leviathans
You fabulous fluked phenomena
Let us in on your knowledge
We were so occupied with our prehensile thumbs
And converting our monkey brains to metaphysics
We never had the time nor concentration
That you were able to devote to pure thought.
We once had a philosopher named Einstein
Who maintained that all things are relative
Einstein! Titans! Do you hear me?

Consider it, you gigantic geniuses
You marvelous monumental mammals
Won't you part with a few clues
A small sample of your vast lore
We were learning to fashion harpoons
And thus had little inclination for ethics
But you floating around and frolicking
Had much leisure for such things.
We once had a philosopher named Melville
Who maintained that you fathomed the secrets of the
    universe
But his name I only whisper to you, whales.

Harold J. Morowitz

THORNTON BEACH

WE ARE ENFOLDED, ENCASED
AND SELF-CREATED
IN A CRAZED
AND LOVELY
sea
of
Chaos
—and enwrapped
and untrapped
in the hand
that holds
the golden flower.
The body sups
on buttercups.
But
the waves!
keep us
raving
with their savory
thunder
and their roaring!

Michael McClure

DEEP CALLETH UNTO DEEP

Old ocean, lulled by thee,
Dream I of eternity!
Leaden wave and leaden sky;
   E'en the stoutest heart stands still
   Feels of ocean-soul the thrill,
As the night-wrack towers high.
In fierce combat now engage
   Demons riding flying clouds;
     Rushing squadrons of the air;
     Cyclone trumpet's awful blare;
   Shrieking of the trembling shrouds;
  Chaos of tumultuous rage!
All-encompassing, stupendous, vast,
Sweeps the horizon round our swaying mast.

Old ocean, lulled by thee,
Dream I of eternity!
Then the calm, with silence shod
   Kissed the billows to repose;
   Fog impenetrable rose;
Shut us in alone with God.
All-encompassing, stupendous, vast,
Sweeps the horizon round our swaying mast!

Old ocean, lulled by thee,
Dream I of eternity!
Lost the land, the sky, the sea;
   Lost the light of sun, of moon;
   Nature failing in a swoon,
Swathed and lost in mystery.
All-encompassing, stupendous, vast,
Sweeps the horizon round our swaying mast!

Old ocean, lulled by thee,
Dream I of eternity!
So the wonders of the deep
   Sank into my very soul,
   Strove to make the heartbreak whole,

As my spirit lay asleep.
All-encompassing, stupendous, vast,
Sweeps the horizon round our swaying mast!

Old ocean, lulled by thee,
Dream I of eternity!
Love's Horizon Infinite,
  Hold, ah, hold in Thine embrace
  Destiny of all our race,
Through the darkness, through the light!
All-encompassing, stupendous, vast,
Sweeps the horizon round our swaying mast!

Henry Nehemiah Dodge

THE EQUINOX

When descends on the Atlantic
   The gigantic
Storm-wind of the equinox,
Landward in his wrath he scourges
   The toiling surges,
Laden with seaweed from the rocks:

From Bermuda's reefs; from edges
   Of sunken ledges,
In some far-off, bright Azore;
From Bahama, and the dashing,
   Silver-flashing
Surges of San Salvador;

From the tumbling surf, that buries
   The Orkneyan skerries,
Answering the hoarse Hebrides;
And from wrecks of ships, and drifting
   Spars, uplifting
On the desolate, rainy seas;—

Ever drifting, drifting, drifting
   On the shifting
Currents of the restless main;
Till in sheltered coves, and reaches
   Of sandy beaches,
All have found repose again.

*From **Seaweed,** Henry Wadsworth Longfellow*

THE BEAUTY OF THE OCEAN

Thee, ocean, once again do I behold
With wild delight, as in the days of old.
The same sensations, yea, the very thoughts
That once were mine in childhood, Time ne'er blots
From memory, but rather doth enhance.
'Tis sweeter now to view thy broad expanse
Of furrow'd waters, far as eye can reach,
To sniff again thine ozone-smelling beach,
And hear thy gentle voice, or thund'rous roar
Upon the pebbly or the rock-bound shore.
'Tis sweeter still to muse on, and to guess
At what and whence thou art who dost impress
Mankind with wonder, awe and sweet delight.
Of God thou surely art, or some dread sprite
Of mystic origin, with power so great,
That thou with ease can'st bear the world's freight,
Can'st play Sky, Sun, and Moon, and catch the tears
Of cloudland through an endless flight of years;
Can'st prove alike to man both friend and foe,
The source of joy and wealth, the cause of woe;
Alike the shield of many a nation's life,
And cause of jealous devastating strife.
What e'er thou art, thou'rt ever fair to view,
Whether in calm thou baskest 'neath the blue
Of Heav'n, or gale-swept, hurl with angry roar
Thy massive white-topped billows on the shore.
I love thee, Ocean! thou hast many friends,
And many too who love for selfish ends.
The merchant loves thee, when thou bring'st him wealth,
The sick man when thou giv'st him back his health.
The sea-gull's grateful for his food and bed,
The mariner and fisherman for bread.
Sea-creatures owe thee thanks for very life,
And naval heroes, victors in the strife;

But th' artist loves with no ulterior end,
And is thy fervent worshipper and friend.
He loves thee for thyself, thy beauties rare;
The poet too, because thou'rt ever fair.

Thomas M. Walker

SUNRISE AT SEA

The quick sea shone
And shivered like spread wings of angels blown
By the sun's breath before him; and a low
Sweet gale shook all the foam-flowers of thin snow
As into rainfall of sea-roses shed
Leaf by wild leaf on that green garden-bed
Which tempests till and sea-winds turn and plough
For rosy and fiery round the running prow
Fluttered the flakes and feathers of the spray,
And bloomed like blossoms cast by God away
To waste on the ardent water; swift the moon
Withered to westward as a face in swoon
Death-stricken by glad tidings: and the height
Throbbed and the centre quivered with delight
And the depth quailed with passion as of love,
Till like the heart of some new-mated dove
Air, light, and wave seemed full of burning rest,
With motion as of one God's beating breast.

Algernon Charles Swinburne

THE SHIPWRECK

Upon the poop the captain stands,
  As starboard as may be;
And pipes on deck the topsail hands
To reef the topsail-gallant strands
  Across the briny sea.

"Ho! splice the anchor under-weigh!"
  The captain loudly cried;
"Ho! lubbers brave, belay! belay!
For we must luff for Falmouth Bay
  Before to-morrow's tide."

The good ship was a racing yawl,
  A spare-rigged schooner sloop,
Athwart the bows the taffrails all
In grummets gay appeared to fall,
  To deck the mainsail poop.

But ere they made the Foreland Light,
  And Deal was left behind,
The wind it blew great gales that night,
And blew the doughty captain tight,
  Full three sheets in the wind.

And right across the tiller head
  The horse it ran apace,
Whereon a traveller hitched and sped
Along the jib and vanished
  To heave the trysail brace.

What ship could live in such a sea?
  What vessel bear the shock?
"Ho! starboard port your helm-a-lee!
Ho! reef the maintop-gallant-tree,
  With many a running block!"

And right upon the Scilly Isles
  The ship had run aground;
When lo! the stalwart Captain Giles
Mounts up upon the gaff and smiles,
  And slews the compass round.

"Saved! saved!" with joy the sailors cry,
  And scandalize the skiff;
As taut and hoisted high and dry
They see the ship unstoppered lie
  Upon the sea-girt cliff.

And since that day in Falmouth Bay,
  As herring-fishers trawl,
The younkers hear the boatswains say
How Captain Giles that awful day
  Preserved the sinking yawl.

E.H. Palmer

SONG OF THE GULF STREAM

'Twas Yesterday He made me and Tomorrow I shall die,
An azure ribbon roaming in my course beneath the sky—
The tomb of old sea rovers, where their bones commingled lie.

You're standing out of Boston, Gloucester, any Eastern
    town—
The spray's akissing rigging and the rollers wash you
    down?
The tops'ls cracking like a gun?—It's time for you to bear
For the stream of purple bubbles and the glories waiting
    there.

My babes are always frolicking and skim the surf along;
The dolphins—twins and triplets—join in Ocean's mighty
    song.
And flashing schools of flying fish the surface deftly clear
When the bow proclaims a holiday and proudly ventures
    near.

With my wandering purple mountains capped with peaks
    of fleecy snow,
And the sunset peering through them, it is then the roamers
    know
Of the land of June eternal and the ballads of the sea—
Little whisperings and beckonings with a spindrift melody.

Where the rolling sun-kissed wool-packs rim the gold
    horizon 'round,
Sending snowy towers and battlements to the zenith with a
    bound,
Where the mellow notes of conches hail the sportive water
    throng
And the roamer's soul is softened by the siren's honeyed
    song—

Then you're sailing in my kingdom and your soul-strings do
   I own,
For although you leave my winey flow, you won't be
   coursing Home
Till you're warming to my heart again and choristers unseen
Give you Welcome to the Glories with the Song of the Gulf
   Stream.

Francis Alan Ford

THE GULF STREAM

They say a tropic river threads the seas
Bearing the strangest things to northern lands:
Vermilion fish, like flowers, with silver bands,
And bronze sea-weed from scarlet coral keys.
Green birds that mock the moon from tall palm trees
Where ghost-gray monkeys hang by cunning hands,
Follow the thinning blue to alien strands
And there among the black pines scream and freeze.
The while this ardent current chills and fails,
Splendors of ice drift slowly south, each one
A frozen torch of borealic fire,
Each one a fairy ship with rainbow sails,
Sinking and fading as it nears the sun
In this relentless river of desire.

Henry Bellamann

NIGHTS ON THE INDIAN OCEAN

Nights on the Indian Ocean,
  Long nights of moon and foam,
When silvery Venus low in the sky
  Follows the sun home.
Long nights when the mild monsoon
  Is breaking south-by-west,
And when soft clouds and the singing shrouds
  Make all that is seem best.

Nights on the Indian Ocean,
  Long nights of space and dream,
When silent Sirius round the Pole
  Swings on, with steady gleam;
When oft the pushing prow
  Seems pressing where before
No prow has ever pressed—or shall
  From hence forevermore.

Nights on the Indian Ocean,
  Long nights—with land at last,
Dim land, dissolving the long sea-spell
  Into a sudden past—
That seems as far away
  As this our life shall seem
When under the shadow of death's shore
  We drop its ended dream.

Cale Young Rice

THE PACIFIC

Fierce courage his and will straight as a Rune,
Who first sailed these vast seas and did not tire.
Unknown to him his haven or his hire,
What reef, what race might wreck him late or soon.
Clear skies above where Venus shone at noon,
Blue waves beneath stained by an Indian dyer;
At night stars dripped from plunging spars like fire,
To wastes of water underneath the moon.
The unknown he explored, home years behind.
And what ahead, oblivious wave, palm isle?
Or, farther still, old loves endeared tenfold?
So sail my soul, a fairer heaven to find,
Whom comfort, safety cannot long beguile,
Seek new gods though you never greet the old.

Percy Stickney Grant

SONG OF THE SEA

The song of the sea was an ancient song
In the days when the earth was young;
The waves were gossiping loud and long
Ere mortals had found a tongue;
The heart of the waves with wrath was wrung
Or soothed to a siren strain,
As they tossed the primitive isles among
Or slept in the open main.
Such was the song and its changes free,
   Such was the song of the sea.

The song of the sea took a human tone
In the days of the coming of man;
A mournfuller meaning swelled her moan,
And fiercer her riots ran;
Because that her stately voice began
To speak of our human woes;
With music mighty to grasp and span
Life's tale and its passion-throes.
Such was the song as it grew to be,
   Such was the song of the sea.

The song of the sea was a hungry sound
As the human years unrolled;
For the notes were hoarse with the doomed
   and drowned,
Or choked with a shipwreck's gold:
Till it seemed no dirge above the mould
So sorry a story said
As the midnight cry of the waters old
Calling above their dead.
Such is the song and its threnody,
   Such is the song of the sea.

The song of the sea is a wondrous lay,
For it mirrors human life,
It is grave and great as the judgment day,
It is torn with the thought of strife;
Yet under the stars it is smooth and rife
With love-lights everywhere,
When the sky has taken the deep to wife
And their wedding-day is fair—
Such is the ocean's mystery,
    Such is the song of the sea.

Richard Burton

THE COAST OF PERU

Come all ye bold sailors
   Who sail round Cape Horn,
Come all ye bold whalers
   Who cruise round for sperm:
The captain has told us,
   An' I hope 'twill prove true,
That there's plenty of sperm whales
   Off the coast of Peru.

The first whale we saw
   Near the close of the day.
Our captain came on deck,
   And thus did he say:
"Now, all my good sailors,
   Pray be of good glee,
For we'll see him in the mornin',
   P'raps under our lee."

It was early next morning,
   Just as the sun rose,
The man at the masthead
   Cried out, " 'Ere she blows!"
"Where away?" cried the captain,
   As he sprang up aloft.
"Three points off our lee bow,
   And scarce two miles off!"

"Now brace up your yard, boys,
   We'll fasten anear,
Get your lines in your boats,
   See your box lines all clear;
Haul back the mainyard, boys,
   Stand by, each boat's crew,
Lower away, lower away,
   My brave fellows, do!

"Now bend to your oars, boys,
   Just make the boat fly,
But whatever you do, boys,
   Keep clear from his eye!"
The first mate soon struck,
   And the whale he went down,
While the old man pulled up,
   And stood by to bend on.

But the whale soon arose,
   To the windward he lay.
We hauled up 'longside
   And he showed us fair play.
We caused him to vomit,
   Thick blood for to spout,
And in less than ten minutes
   We rolled him fin out.

We towed him alongside
   With many a shout,
That day cut him in
   And began to boil out.
Oh, now he's all boiled out
   And stowed down below,
And we're waiting to hear 'em
   Sing out "'Ere she blows!"

Anonymous

OF THE SEA, A SONG

But once, oh God, a song comes from my lips
That only clac had framed a curse
What time mine eyes have aching scanned the expanse
Of blue-green ocean. This sole chant
Is drawn from stained and unaccustomed lips
Unused to song.

The seas are deep, too deep to move
When falls a solitary human tear:
No sob is heard above the insistent roar
Of waters hiding deep what will not drown;
Hence once, in this great once, I sing,
And as a song must ever be
Gladsome, for singing, through the breeze
This one clear song comes up from me.
—Those waves!
You say they dance, they frivol, froth and fall
—My Lad!—Those waters, heaping there,
Tell one glad thing, colossal good for us;
There's humans in the paradise
Repenting fast, and—hear that sob?
Hm! yes, you heard it: sobs, great tears
Falling and cleansing all the air,
Human, around us. Smell o' salt?
Aye, they are bitter tears.

E.A. Fielder

THE TRACKLESS DEEPS

Those trackless deeps, where many a weary sail
Has seen, above the illimitable plain,
Morning and night, and night on morning rise;
Whilst still no land to greet the wanderer spread
Its shadowy mountains on the sun-bright sea,
Where the loud roaring of the tempest-waves
So long have mingled with the gusty wind
In melancholy loneliness, and swept
The desert of those ocean solitudes;
But, vocal to the sea-bird's harrowing shriek,
The bellowing monster and the rushing storm,
Now to the sweet and many-mingling sounds
Of kindliest human impulses respond.

Percy Bysshe Shelley

THE CREATION OF THE SEA

Over all the face of Earth
Main ocean flowed, not idle, but, with warm
Prolific humour softening all her globe,
Fermented the great mother to conceive,
Satiate with genial moisture; when God said,
"Be gathered now, ye waters under heaven,
Into one place, and let dry land appear!"
Immediately the mountains huge appear
Emergent, and their broad bare backs upheave
Into the clouds; their tops ascend the sky.
So high as heaved the tumid hills, so low
Down sunk a hollow bottom broad and deep,
Capacious bed of waters. Thither they
Hasted with glad precipitance, uprolled,
As drops on dust conglobing, from the dry:
Part rise in crystal wall, or ridge direct,
For haste; such flight the great command impressed
On the swift floods. As armies at the call
Of trumpet (for of armies thou hast heard)
Troop to the standard, so the watery throng,
Wave rolling after wave, where way they found—
If steep, with torrent rapture, if through plain,
Soft-ebbing; nor withstood them rock or hill;
But they, or underground, or circuit wide
With serpent error wandering, found their way,
And on the washy ooze deep channels wore:
Easy, ere God had bid the ground be dry,
All but within those banks where rivers now
Stream, and perpetual draw their humid train.
The dry land Earth, and the great receptacle
Of congregated waters He called Seas.

*From **Paradise Lost**, John Milton*

PSALM CVII

Verses 23. . . 30

They that go down to the sea in ships, that do business
    in great waters;
These see the works of the Lord, and his wonders
    in the deep.
For he commandeth, and raiseth the stormy wind, which
    lifteth up the waves thereof.
They mount up to the heaven, they go down again to the
    depths: their soul is melted because of trouble.
They reel to and fro, and stagger like a drunken man,
    and are at their wit's end.
Then they cry unto the Lord in their trouble,
    and he bringeth them out of their distresses.
He maketh the storm a calm, so that the waves
    thereof are still.
Then are they glad because they be quiet; so he bringeth
    them unto their desired haven.

SHAKESPEARE ON THE SEA

Thou God of this great vast, rebuke these surges,
Which wash both heaven and hell; and Thou that hast
Upon the winds command, bind them in brass,
Having call'd them from the deep! O, still
Thy deafening, dreadful thunders; gently quench
Thy nimble, sulphurous flashes!
           Thou stormest venomously;
Wilt thou spit all thyself? The seaman's whistle
Is as a whisper in the ears of death,
Unheard.

*From **Pericles**, William Shakespeare*

THE SECRET OF THE SEA

Who knows the mighty secret,
The secret of the sea?
I love its beauty passing well,
I love the thunder of its swell,
I love the glory of its play,
The glitter of its feathery spray,
But its secret is hid from me.

Who knows the mighty secret—
What gives the sea its power?
Its laugh will chime with the gayest mood,
It gives the friend to solitude;
It frets with the fretted heart or head,
It mourns the past, it wails the dead,
It lulls the dreamy hour.

Who has the mighty secret?
Never a mortal knows.
By the shells alone is the riddle read,
As they lie deep down in their coral bed,
In the depths of the seaweed forest brown,
Where the August sunshine quivers down,
And the great tide comes and goes.

They know the mighty secret;
They are cast upon the sand;
We gather them up from the creamy foam,
We bear them away to our inland home,
As relics of happy seaside days,
We bear them to dwell where the soft breeze plays
Over the flowery land.

They know the mighty secret;
They murmur it all day long.
With a passionate wail, with a yearning cry,
For the shadowy reef where the surf beats high,
Where the great waves roll for ever and aye,
And their roar swells up to the hanging sky,
And the wind blows wild and strong.

They know the mighty secret;
We hold them to our ear,
We hear the mystical sound again,
We hear the voice of the restless main,
We know the long monotonous roar,
As the billows break on the rugged shore;
But that is all we hear.

We cannot read the secret,
We cannot find the key.
Ah! sully not by earthly guess
Its grandeur and its loveliness;
Take the infinite gladness of the main,
And fling the poor shell back again,
Back to its parent sea.

Susan K. Phillips

BYRON'S ADDRESS TO THE OCEAN

Roll on, thou deep and dark blue Ocean—roll!
Ten thousand fleets sweep over thee in vain;
Man marks the earth with ruin—his control
Stops with the shore;—upon the watery plain
The wrecks are all thy deed, nor doth remain
A shadow of man's ravage, save his own,
When, for a moment, like a drop of rain,
He sinks into thy depths with bubbling groan,
Without a grave, unknelled, uncoffined, and unknown.

His steps are not thy paths, thy fields
Are not a spoil for him,—thou dost arise
And shake him from thee; the vile strength he wields
For earth's destruction thou dost all despise,
Spurning him from thy bosom to the skies,
And send'st him, shivering in thy playful spray
And howling, to his gods, where haply lies
His petty hope in some near port or bay,
And dashest him again to earth:—there let him lay.

The armaments which thunder-strike the walls
Of rock-built cities, bidding nations quake,
And monarchs tremble in their capitals,
The oak leviathans, whose huge ribs make
Their clay creator the vain title take
Of lord of thee, and arbiter of war;
These are thy toys, and, as the snowy flake,
They melt into thy yeast of waves, which mar
Alike the Armada's pride or spoils of Trafalgar.

Thy shores are empires, changed in all save thee—
Assyria, Greece, Rome, Carthage, what are they?
Thy waters washed them power while they were free,
And many a tyrant since; their shores obey
The stranger, slave, or savage; their decay
Has dried up realms to deserts:—not so thou;—
Unchangeable save to thy wild waves' play—
Time writes no wrinkle on thine azure brow—
Such as creation's dawn beheld, thou rollest now.

Thou glorious mirror, where the Almighty's form
Glasses itself in tempests; in all time,
Calm or convulsed—in breeze, or gale, or storm,
Icing the pole, or in the torrid clime
Dark-heaving;—boundless, endless, and sublime—
The image of Eternity—the throne
Of the Invisible; even from out thy slime
The monsters of the deep are made: each zone
Obeys thee: thou goest forth, dread, fathomless, alone.

And I have loved thee, Ocean! and my joy
Of youthful sports was on thy breast to be
Borne, like thy bubbles, onward: from a boy
I wantoned with thy breakers—they to me
Were a delight; and if the freshening sea
Made them a terror—'twas a pleasing fear,
For I was as it were a child of thee,
And trusted to thy billows far and near,
And laid my hand upon thy mane—as I do here.

Lord Byron

ON THE SEA

It keeps eternal whisperings around
   Desolate shores, and with its mighty swell
   Gluts twice ten thousand caverns, till the spell
Of Hecate leaves them their old shadowy sound.
Often 'tis in such gentle temper found,
   That scarcely will the very smallest shell
   Be mov'd for days from whence it sometime fell.
When last the winds of heaven were unbound.

Oh ye! who have your eye-balls vex'd and tired,
   Feast them upon the wideness of the Sea;
Oh ye! whose ears are dinn'd with uproar rude,
   Or fed too much with cloying melody,—
Sit ye near some old cavern's mouth, and brood
Until ye start, as if the sea-nymphs quired!

John Keats

IS MY LOVER ON THE SEA?

Is my lover on the sea,
    Sailing east, or sailing west?
Mighty Ocean, gentle be,
    Rock him into rest!

Let no angry wind arise,
    Nor a wave with whitened crest;
All be gentle as his eyes
    When he is caressed!

Bear him (as the breeze above
    Bears the bird unto its nest)
Here—unto his home of love,
    And there bid him rest!

Barry Cornwall

BLACK-EYED SUSAN

All in the Downs the fleet was moored,
  The streamers waving in the wind,
When black-eyed Susan came on board:
  "Oh! where shall I my true love find?
Tell me, ye jovial sailors, tell me true,
If my sweet William sails among your crew?"

William, who, high upon the yard,
  Rock'd by the billows to and fro,
Soon as her well-known voice he heard,
  He sighed and cast his eyes below:
The cord glides swiftly through his glowing hands,
And quick as lightning on the deck he stands.

So the sweet lark, high-poised in air,
  Shuts close his pinions to his breast
If chance his mate's shrill call he hear,
  And drops at once into her nest:—
The noblest captain in the British fleet
Might envy William's lips those kisses sweet.

"O Susan, Susan, lovely dear,
  My vows shall ever true remain!
Let me kiss off that falling tear,—
  We only part to meet again:
Change as ye list, ye winds, my heart shall be
The faithful compass that still points to thee!

"Believe not what the landsmen say,
  Who tempt, with doubts, thy constant mind:
They'll tell thee, sailors, when away,
  In every port a mistress find.—
Yes, yes!—believe them when they tell thee so
For thou art present wheresoe'er I go!

"If to fair India's coast we sail,
    Thine eyes are seen in diamonds bright;
Thy breath is Afric's spicy gale,—
    Thy skin is ivory so white:
Thus every beauteous object that I view
Wakes in my soul some charm of lovely Sue.

"Though battle calls me from thy arms,
    Let not my pretty Susan mourn;
Though cannons roar, yet, free from harms,
    William shall to his dear return:
Love turns aside the balls that round me fly,
Lest precious tears should drop from Susan's eye."

The boatswain gives his dreadful word,—
    The sails their swelling bosoms spread;
No longer may she stay on board:
    They kiss: She sighs: He hangs his head.
Her lessening boat unwilling rows to land:
"Adieu!" she cries, and waves her lily hand.

John Gay

A SAILOR'S YARN

As narrated by the second mate to one of the marines

This is the tale that was told to me,
By a battered and shattered son of the sea:
To me and my messmate, Silas Green,
When I was a guileless young marine.

" 'T was the good ship 'Gyacutus,'
All in the China seas;
With the wind a lee, and the capstan free,
To catch the summer breeze.

" 'T was Captain Porgie on the deck
To the mate in the mizzen hatch,
While the boatswain bold, in the for'ard hold,
Was winding his larboard watch.

" 'Oh, how does our good ship head to-night?
How heads our gallant craft?'
'Oh, she heads to the E.S.W. by N.
And the binnacle lies abaft.'

" 'Oh, what does the quadrant indicate?
And how does the sextant stand?'
'Oh, the sextant's down to the freezing point
And the quadrant's lost a hand.'

" 'Oh, if the quadrant's lost a hand,
And the sextant falls so low,
It's our body and bones to Davy Jones
This night are bound to go.

" 'Oh, fly aloft to the garboard-strake,
And reef the spanker boom,
Bend a stubbing sail on the martingale
To give her weather room.

" 'Oh, boatswain, down in the for'ard hold
What water do you find?'
'Four foot and half by the royal gaff
And rather more behind.'

" 'Oh, sailors, collar your marline spikes
And each belaying pin;
Come, stir your stumps to spike the pumps,
Or more will be coming in.'

" 'They stirred their stumps, they spiked the pumps
They spliced the mizzen brace;
Aloft and alow they worked, but, oh!
The water gained apace.

"They bored a hole below her line
To let the water out,
But more and more with awful roar
The water in did spout.

"Then up spoke the cook of our gallant ship—
And he was a lubber brave—
'I've several wives in various ports,
And my life I'd like to save.'

"Then up spoke the captain of marines,
Who dearly loved his prog:
'It's awful to die, and it's worse to be dry,
And I move we pipes to grog.'

"Oh, then 't was the gallant second-mate
As stopped them sailors' jaw,
'T was the second-mate whose hand had weight
In laying down the law.

"He took the anchor on his back,
And leapt into the main;
Through foam and spray he clove his way,
And sunk, and rose again.

"Through foam and spray a league away
The anchor stout he bore,
Till, safe at last, I made it fast,
And warped the ship ashore."

This is the tale that was told to me,
By that modest and truthful son of the sea.
And I envy the life of a second mate,
Though captains curse him and sailors hate;
For he ain't like some of the swabs I've seen,
As would go and lie to a poor marine.

J.J. Roche

THE ALARMED SKIPPER

Many a long, long year ago,
Nantucket skippers had a plan
Of finding out, though "lying low,"
How near New York their schooners ran.

They greased the lead before it fell,
And then, by sounding through the night,—
Knowing the soil that stuck, so well,
They always guessed their reckoning right.

A skipper gray, whose eyes were dim,
Could tell, by *tasting*, just the spot,
And so below he'd "dowse the glim"—
After, of course, his "something hot."

Snug in his berth, at eight o'clock,
This ancient skipper might be found;
No matter how his craft would rock,
He slept,—for skippers' naps are sound!

The watch on deck would now and then
Run down and wake him, with the lead;—
He'd up, and taste, and tell the men
How many miles they went ahead.

One night, 'twas Jotham Marden's watch,
A curious wag,—the peddler's son,—
And so he mused, (the wanton wretch),
"Tonight I'll have a grain of fun.

"We're all a set of stupid fools
To think the skipper knows by *tasting*
What ground he's on; Nantucket schools
Don't teach such stuff, with all their basting!"

And so he took the well-greased lead
And rubbed it o'er a box of earth
That stood on deck,—a parsnip-bed,—
And then he sought the skipper's berth.

"Where are we now, Sir? Please to taste."
The skipper yawned, put out his tongue,
Then oped his eyes in wondrous haste,
And then upon the floor he sprung!

The skipper stormed, and tore his hair,
Thrust on his boots, and roared to Marden,
"Nantucket's sunk, and here we are
Right over old Marm Hackett's garden!"

James T. Fields

THE SAILOR TO HIS PARROT

Thou foul-mouthed wretch! Why dost thou choose
   To learn bad language, and no good;
Canst thou not say 'The Lord be praised'
   As easy as 'Hell's fire and blood'?

Why didst thou call the gentle priest
   A thief and a damned rogue; and tell
The deacon's wife, who came to pray,
   To hold her jaw and go to hell?

Thou art a foe, no friend of mine,
   For all my thoughts thou givest away;
Whate'er I say in confidence,
   Thou dost in evil hours betray.

Thy mind's for ever set on bad;
   I cannot mutter one small curse,
But thou dost make it endless song,
   And shout it to a neighbour's house.

Aye, swear to thy delight and ours,
   When here I welcome shipmates home,
And thou canst see abundant grog—
   But hold thy tongue when landsmen come.

Be dumb when widow Johnson's near,
   Be dumb until our wedding day;
And after that—but not before—
   She will enjoy the worst you say.

There is a time to speak and not;
   When we're together, all is well;
But damn thy soul—What! you damn *mine!*
   And you tell *me* to go to hell!

W.H. Davies

THE SEA-KING

From out his castle on the sand
He led his tawny-bearded band
In stormy bark from land to land.

The red dawn was his goodly sign:
He set his face to sleet and brine,
And quaffed the blast like ruddy wine.

And often felt the swirling gale
Beat, like some giant thresher's flail,
Upon his battered coat of mail.

Or sacked, at times, some windy town,
And from the pastures, parched and brown,
He drove the scurrying cattle down;

And kissed the maids, and stole the bell
From off the church below the fell,
And drowned the priest within the well.

And he had seen, on frosty nights,
Strange, whirling forms and elfin sights,
In twilight land, by Northern Lights.

Or, sailing on by windless shoal,
Had heard, by night, the song of troll
Within some cavern-haunted knoll.

Off Iceland, too, the sudden rush
Of waters falling, in a hush
He heard the ice-fields grind and crush.

His prow the shining south seas clove;
Warm, spiced winds from lemon-grove
And heated thicket round him drove.

The storm-blast was his deity;
His lover was the fitful sea;
The wailing winds his melody.

By rocky scaur and beachy head
He followed where his fancy led,
And down the rainy waters fled;

And left the peopled towns behind,
And gave his days and nights to find
What lay beyond the western wind.

L. Frank Tooker

THE PHANTOM SHIP

In Mather's Magnalia Christi,
  Of the old colonial time,
May be found in prose the legend
  That is here set down in rhyme.

A ship sailed from New Haven,
  And the keen and frosty airs,
That filled her sails at parting,
  Were heavy with good men's prayers.

"O Lord! if it be thy pleasure"—
  Thus prayed the old divine—
"To bury our friends in the ocean,
  Take them, for they are thine!"

But Master Lamberton muttered,
  And under his breath said he,
"This ship is so crank and walty
  I fear our grave she will be!"

And the ships that came from England,
  When the winter months were gone,
Brought no tidings of this vessel
  Nor of Master Lamberton.

This put the people to praying
  That the Lord would let them hear
What in his greater wisdom
  He had done with friends so dear.

And at last their prayers were answered:—
  It was in the month of June,
An hour before the sunset
  Of a windy afternoon,

When, steadily steering landward,
  A ship was seen below,
And they knew it was Lamberton, Master,
  Who sailed so long ago.

On she came, with a cloud of canvas,
  Right against the wind that blew,
Until the eye could distinguish
  The faces of the crew.

Then fell her straining topmasts,
  Hanging tangled in the shrouds,
And her sails were loosened and lifted,
  And blown away like clouds.

And the masts, with all their rigging,
  Fell slowly, one by one,
And the hulk dilated and vanished,
  As a sea-mist in the sun!

And the people who saw this marvel
  Each said unto his friend,
That this was the mould of their vessel,
  And thus her tragic end.

And the pastor of the village
  Gave thanks to God in prayer,
That, to quiet their troubled spirits,
  He had sent this Ship of Air.

Henry Wadsworth Longfellow

COLUMBUS

Once upon a time there was an Italian,
And some people thought he was a rapscallion,
But he wasn't offended,
Because other people thought he was splendid,
And he said the world was round,
And everybody made an uncomplimentary sound,
But he went and tried to borrow some money
   from Ferdinand
But Ferdinand said America was a bird in the bush
   and he'd rather have a berdinand,
But Columbus' brain was fertile, it wasn't arid,
And he remembered that Ferdinand was married,
And he thought, there is no wife like a misunderstood one,
Because if her husband thinks something is a terrible idea
   she is bound to think it a good one,
So he perfumed his handkerchief with bay rum
   and citronella,
And he went to see Isabella,
And he looked wonderful but he had never felt sillier,
And she said, I can't place the face but the aroma is familiar,
And Columbus didn't say a word,
All he said was, I am Columbus, the fifteenth-century
   Admiral Byrd,
And, just as he thought, her disposition was very malleable,
And she said, Here are my jewels, and she wasn't penuri-
   ous like Cornelia the mother of Gracchi, she wasn't re-
   ferring to her children, no, she was referring to her
   jewels, which were very very valuable,
So Columbus said, Somebody show me the sunset
   and somebody did and he set sail for it,
And he discovered America and they put him in jail for it,
And the fetters gave him welts,
And they named America after somebody else,
So the sad fate of Columbus ought to be pointed out
   to every child and every voter,
Because it has a very important moral, which is, Don't be a
   discoverer, be a promoter.

ABOARD AT A SHIP'S HELM

Aboard at a ship's helm,
A young steersman steering with care.
Through fog on a sea-coast dolefully ringing,
An ocean-bell—O a warning bell, rock'd by the waves.
O you give good notice indeed, you bell by the sea-reefs
    ringing,
Ringing, ringing, to warn the ship from its wreck-place.

For as on the alert O steersman, you mind the loud
    admonition,
The bows turn, the freighted ship tacking speeds away
    under her gray sails,
The beautiful and noble ship with all her precious wealth
    speeds away gayly and safe.
But O the ship, the immortal ship! O ship aboard the ship!
Ship of the body, ship of the soul, voyaging, voyaging,
    voyaging.

Walt Whitman

DOVER BEACH

The sea is calm to-night.
The tide is full, the moon lies fair
Upon the straits;—on the French coast the light
Gleams and is gone; the cliffs of England stand
Glimmering and vast, out in the tranquil bay.

Come to the window, sweet is the night-air!
Only, from the long line of spray
Where the sea meets the moon-blanch'd land,
Listen! you hear the grating roar
Of pebbles which the waves draw back, and fling,
At their return, up the high strand.
Begin, and cease, and then again begin,
With tremulous cadence slow, and bring
The eternal note of sadness in.

Sophocles long ago
Heard it on the Aegean, and it brought
Into his mind the turbid ebb and flow,
Of human misery; we
Find also in the sound a thought,
Hearing it by this distant northern sea.

The Sea of Faith
Was once, too, at the full, and round earth's shore
Lay like the folds of a bright girdle furl'd.
But now I only hear
Its melancholy, long, withdrawing roar,
Retreating, to the breath
Of the night-wind, down the vast edges drear
And naked shingles of the world.

Ah, love, let us be true
To one another! for the world, which seems
To lie before us like a land of dreams,
So various, so beautiful, so new,

Hath really neither joy, nor love, nor light,
Nor certitude, nor peace, nor help for pain;
And we are here as on a darkling plain
Swept with confused alarms of struggle and flight,
Where ignorant armies clash by night.

Matthew Arnold

SIR JOSEPH'S SONG

When I was a lad I served a term
As office boy to an Attorney's firm.
I cleaned the windows and I swept the floor,
And I polished up the handle of the big front door.
   I polished up that handle so carefullee
   That now I am the Ruler of the Queen's Navee!

As office boy I made such a mark
That they gave me the post of a junior clerk.
I served the writs with a smile so bland,
And I copied all the letters in a big round hand—
   I copied all the letters in a hand so free,
   That now I am the Ruler of the Queen's Navee!

In serving writs I made such a name
That an articled clerk I soon became;
I wore clean collars and a brand new suit
For the pass examination at the Institute,
   And that pass examination did so well for me,
   That now I am the Ruler of the Queen's Navee!

Of legal knowledge I acquired such a grip
That they took me into the partnership.
And that junior partnership, I ween,
Was the only ship that I ever had seen.
   But that kind of ship so suited me,
   That now I am the Ruler of the Queen's Navee!

I grew so rich that I was sent
By a pocket borough into Parliament.
I always voted at my party's call,
And I never thought of thinking for myself at all.
   I thought so little, they rewarded me
   By making me the Ruler of the Queen's Navee!

Now Landsmen all, whoever you may be,
If you want to rise to the top of the tree,
If your soul isn't fettered to an office stool,
Be careful to be guided by this golden rule—
    Stick close to your desks and never go to sea,
    And you all may be Rulers of the Queen's Navee!

From **H.M.S. Pinafore,** *W.S. Gilbert*

THE WALRUS AND THE CARPENTER

The sun was shining on the sea,
  Shining with all his might:
He did his very best to make
  The billows smooth and bright—
And this was odd, because it was
  The middle of the night.

The moon was shining sulkily,
  Because she thought the sun
Had got no business to be there
  After the day was done—
'It's very rude of him,' she said,
  'To come and spoil the fun!'

The sea was wet as wet could be,
  The sands were dry as dry.
You could not see a cloud, because
  No cloud was in the sky:
No birds were flying overhead—
  There were no birds to fly.

The Walrus and the Carpenter
  Were walking close at hand:
They wept like anything to see
  Such quantities of sand:
'If this were only cleared away,'
  They said, 'it *would* be grand!'

'If seven maids with seven mops
  Swept it for half a year,
Do you suppose,' the Walrus said,
  'That they could get it clear?'
'I doubt it,' said the Carpenter,
  And shed a bitter tear.

'O Oysters, come and walk with us!'
  The Walrus did beseech.
'A pleasant walk, a pleasant talk,
  Along the briny beach:
We cannot do with more than four,
  To give a hand to each.'

The eldest Oyster looked at him,
  But never a word he said:
The eldest Oyster winked his eye,
  And shook his heavy head—
Meaning to say he did not choose
  To leave the oyster-bed.

But four young Oysters hurried up,
  All eager for the treat:
Their coats were brushed, their faces washed,
  Their shoes were clean and neat—
And this was odd, because, you know,
  They hadn't any feet.

Four other Oysters followed them,
  And yet another four;
And thick and fast they came at last,
  And more, and more, and more—
All hopping through the frothy waves,
  And scrambling to the shore.

The Walrus and the Carpenter
  Walked on a mile or so,
And then they rested on a rock
  Conveniently low:
And all the little Oysters stood
  And waited in a row.

'The time has come,' the Walrus said,
    To talk of many things:
Of shoes—and ships—and sealing wax—
    Of cabbages—and kings—
And why the sea is boiling hot—
    And whether pigs have wings.'

'But wait a bit,' the Oysters cried,
    'Before we have our chat;
For some of us are out of breath,
    And all of us are fat!'
'No hurry!' said the Carpenter.
    They thanked him much for that.

'A loaf of bread,' the Walrus said,
    'Is what we chiefly need:
Pepper and vinegar besides
    Are very good indeed—
Now, if you're ready, Oysters dear,
    We can begin to feed.'

'But not on us!' the Oysters cried,
    Turning a little blue.
'After such kindness, that would be
    A dismal thing to do!'
'The night is fine,' the Walrus said.
    'Do you admire the view?'

'It was so kind of you to come!
    And you are very nice!'
The Carpenter said nothing but
    'Cut us another slice.
I wish you were not quite so deaf—
    I've had to ask you twice!'

'It seems a shame,' the Walrus said,
    'To play them such a trick.
After we've brought them out so far,
    And made them trot so quick!'
The Carpenter said nothing but
    'The butter's spread too thick!'

'I weep for you,' the Walrus said:
    'I deeply sympathize.'
With sobs and tears he sorted out
    Those of the largest size,
Holding his pocket-handkerchief
    Before his streaming eyes.

'O Oysters,' said the Carpenter.
    'You've had a pleasant run!
Shall we be trotting home again?'
    But answer came there none—
And this was scarcely odd, because
    They'd eaten every one.

Lewis Carroll

AN OLD SONG RE-SUNG

I saw a ship a-sailing, a-sailing, a-sailing,
With emeralds and rubies and sapphires in her hold;
And a bosun in a blue coat bawling at the railing,
Piping through a silver call that had a chain of gold;
The summer wind was falling and the tall ship rolled.

I saw a ship a-steering, a-steering, a-steering,
With roses in red thread worked upon her sails;
With sacks of purple amethysts, the spoils of buccaneering,
Skins of musky yellow wine, and silks in bales,
Her merry men were cheering, hauling in the brails.

I saw a ship a-sinking, a-sinking, a-sinking,
With glittering sea-water splashing on her decks,
With seamen in her spirit-room singing songs and drinking,
Pulling claret bottles down, and knocking off the necks,
The broken glass was chinking as she sank among
   the wrecks.

John Masefield

BOATS IN A FOG

Sports and gallantries, the stage, the arts, the antics
    of dancers,
The exuberant voices of music,
Have charm for children but lack nobility; it is bitter
    earnestness
That makes beauty; the mind
Knows, grown adult.
           A sudden fog-drift muffled the ocean,
A throbbing of engines moved in it,
At length, a stone's throw out, between the rocks and
    the vapor,
One by one moved shadows
Out of the mystery, shadows, fishing-boats, trailing each
    other
Following the cliff for guidance,
Holding a difficult path between the peril of the sea-fog
And the foam on the shore granite.
One by one, trailing their leader, six crept by me,
Out of the vapor and into it,
The throb of their engines subdued by the fog, patient
    and cautious,
Coasting all round the peninsula
Back to the buoys in Monterey harbor. A flight of pelicans
Is nothing lovelier to look at;
The flight of the planets is nothing nobler; all the arts
    lose virtue
Against the essential reality
Of creatures going about their business among the equally
Earnest elements of nature.

Robinson Jeffers

CHOOSING A MAST

This mast, new-shaved, through whom I rive the ropes,
Says she was once an oread of the slopes,
Graceful and tall upon the rocky highlands,
A slender tree as vertical as noon,
And her low voice was lovely as the silence
Through which a fountain whistles to the moon,
Who now of the white spray must take the veil
And, for her songs, the thunder of the sail.

I chose her for her fragrance, when the spring
With sweetest resins swelled her fourteenth ring
And with live amber welded her young thews:
I chose her for the glory of the Muse,
Smoother of forms that her hard-knotted grain,
Grazed by the chisel, shaven by the plane,
Might from the steel as cool a burnish take
As from the bladed moon a windless lake.

I chose her for her eagerness of flight
Where she stood tiptoe on the rocky height
Lifted by her own perfume to the sun,
While through her rustling plumes with eager sound
Her eagle spirit, with the gale at one,
Spreading wide pinions, would have spurned the ground
And her own sleeping shadow, had they not
With thymy fragrance charmed her to the spot.

Lover of song, I chose this mountain pine
Not only for the straightness of her spine
But for her songs: for there she loved to sing
Through a long noon's repose of wave and wing,
The fluvial swirling of her scented hair
Sole rill of song in all that windless air,
And her slim form the naiad of the stream
Afloat upon the languor of its theme;

And for the soldier's fare on which she fed:
Her wine the azure, and the snow her bread;
And for her stormy watches on the height,
For only out of solitude or strife
Are born the sons of valour and delight;
And lastly for her rich exulting life,
That with the wind stopped not its singing breath
But carolled on, the louder for its death.

Under a pine, when summer days were deep,
We loved the most to lie in love or sleep;
And when in long hexameters the west
Rolled his grey surge, the forest for his lyre,
It was the pines that sang us to our rest,
Loud in the wind and fragrant in the fire,
With legioned voices swelling all night long,
From Pelion to Provence, their storm of song.

It was the pines that fanned us in the heat,
The pines, that cheered us in the time of sleet,
For which sweet gifts I set one dryad free;
No longer to the wind a rooted foe,
This nymph shall wander where she longs to be
And with the blue north wind arise and go,
A silver huntress with the moon to run
And fly through rainbows with the rising sun;

And when to pasture in the glittering shoals
The guardian mistral drives his thundering foals,
And when like Tartar horsemen racing free
We ride the snorting fillies of the sea,
My pine shall be the archer of the gale
While on the bending willow curves the sail
From whose great bow the long keel shooting home
Shall fly, the feathered arrow of the foam.

Roy Campbell

TO THE HARBORMASTER

I wanted to be sure to reach you;
though my ship was on the way it got caught
in some moorings. I am always tying up
and then deciding to depart. In storms and
at sunset, with the metallic coils of the tide
around my fathomless arms, I am unable
to understand the forms of my vanity
or I am hard alee with my Polish rudder
in my hand and the sun sinking. To
you I offer my hull and the tattered cordage
of my will. The terrible channels where
the wind drives me against the brown lips
of the reeds are not all behind me. Yet
I trust the sanity of my vessel; and
if it sinks, it may well be in answer
to the reasoning of the eternal voices,
the waves which have kept me from reaching you.

Frank O'Hara

A VALEDICTION

We're bound for blue water where the great winds blow,
It's time to get the tacks aboard, time for us to go;
The crowd's at the capstan and the tune's in the shout,
'A long pull, a strong pull, *and warp the hooker out.*'

The bow-wash is eddying, spreading from the bows,
Aloft and loose the topsails and some one give a rouse;
A salt Atlantic chanty shall be music to the dead,
'A long pull, a strong pull, *and the yard to the masthead.*'

Green and merry run the seas, the wind comes cold,
Salt and strong and pleasant, and worth a mint of gold;
And she's staggering, swooping, as she feels her feet,
'A long pull, a strong pull, *and aft the main-sheet.*'

Shrilly squeal the running sheaves, the weather-gear
    strains,
Such a clatter of chain-sheets, the devil's in the chains;
Over us the bright stars, under us the drowned,
'A long pull, a strong pull, *and we're outward bound.*'

Yonder, round and ruddy, is the mellow old moon,
The red-funnelled tug has gone, and now, sonny, soon
We'll be clear of the Channel, so watch how you steer,
'Ease her when she pitches, *and so-long, my dear.*'

John Masefield

A WANDERER'S SONG

A wind's in the heart of me, a fire's in my heels,
I am tired of brick and stone and rumbling wagon-wheels;
I hunger for the sea's edge, the limits of the land,
Where the wild old Atlantic is shouting on the sand.

Oh I'll be going, leaving the noises of the street,
To where a lifting foresail-foot is yanking at the sheet;
To a windy, tossing anchorage where yawls and ketches
   ride,
Oh I'll be going, going, until I meet the tide.

And first I'll hear the sea-wind, the mewing of the gulls,
The clucking, sucking of the sea about the rusty hulls,
The songs at the capstan in the hooker warping out,
And then the heart of me'll know I'm there or thereabout.

Oh I am tired of brick and stone, the heart of me is sick,
For windy green, unquiet sea, the realm of Moby Dick;
And I'll be going, going, from the roaring of the wheels,
For a wind's in the heart of me, a fire's in my heels.

John Masefield

THE TARRY BUCCANEER

I'm going to be a pirate with a bright brass pivot-gun,
And an island in the Spanish Main beyond the setting sun,
And a silver flagon full of red wine to drink when work
    is done,
    Like a fine old salt-sea scavenger, like a tarry Buccaneer.

With a sandy creek to careen in, and a pig-tailed Spanish
    mate,
And under my main-hatches a sparkling merry freight
Of doubloons and double moidores and pieces of eight,
    Like a fine old salt-sea scavenger, like a tarry Buccaneer.

With a taste for Spanish wine-shops and for spending my
    doubloons,
And a crew of swart mulattoes and black-eyed octoroons,
And a thoughtful way with mutineers of making them
    maroons,
    Like a fine old salt-sea scavenger, like a tarry Buccaneer.

With a sash of crimson velvet and a diamond-hilted sword,
And a silver whistle about my neck secured to a golden
    cord,
And a habit of taking captives and walking them along
    a board,
    Like a fine old salt-sea scavenger, like a tarry Buccaneer.

With a spy-glass tucked beneath my arm and a cocked hat
    cocked askew,
And a long low rakish schooner a-cutting of the waves
    in two,
And a flag of skull and cross-bones the wickedest that ever
    flew,
    Like a fine old salt-sea scavenger, like a tarry Buccaneer.

John Masefield

THE SHIP AND HER MAKERS

THE ORE

Before Man's labouring wisdom gave me birth
I had not even seen the light of day;
Down in the central darkness of the earth,
Crushed by the weight of continents I lay,
Ground by the weight to heat, not knowing then
The Air, the light, the noise, the world of men.

THE TREES

We grew on mountains where the glaciers cry,
Infinite sombre armies of us stood
Below the snow-peaks which defy the sky;
A song like the gods moaning filled our wood;
We knew no men—our life was to stand staunch,
Singing our song, against the avalanche.

THE HEMP AND FLAX

We were a million grasses on the hill,
A million herbs which bowed as the wind blew,
Trembling in every fibre, never still;
Out of the summer earth sweet life we drew.
Little blue-flowered grasses up the glen,
Glad of the sun, what did we know of men?

THE WORKERS

We tore the iron from the mountain's hold,
By blasting fires we smithied it to steel;
Out of the shapeless stone we learned to mould
The sweeping bow, the rectilinear keel;
We hewed the pine to plank, we split the fir,
We pulled the myriad flax to fashion her.

Out of a million lives our knowledge came,
A million subtle craftsmen forged the means;
Steam was our handmaid and our servant flame,
Water our strength, all bowed to our machines.
Out of the rock, the tree, the springing herb
We built this wandering beauty so superb.

THE SAILORS

We, who were born on earth and live by air,
Make this thing pass across the fatal floor,
The speechless sea; alone we commune there
Jesting with death, that ever open door.
Sun, moon and stars are signs by which we drive
This wind-blown iron like a thing alive.

THE SHIP

I march across great waters like a queen,
I whom so many wisdoms helped to make;
Over the uncruddled billows of seas green
I blanch the bubbled highway of my wake.
By me my wandering tenants clasp the hands,
And know the thoughts of men in other lands.

John Masefield

REQUIEM

Under the wide and starry sky,
Dig the grave and let me lie.
Glad did I live and gladly die,
   And I lay me down with a will.

This be the verse you grave for me:
"Here he lies where he longed to be;
Home is the sailor, home from the sea,
   And the hunter home from the hill."

Robert Louis Stevenson

INDEX OF TITLES

A Life on the Ocean Wave	5
A Sailor's Song	15
A Sailor's Yarn	137
A Sea Dirge	35
A Valediction	162
A Wanderer's Song	163
A Wet Sheet and a Flowing Sea	6
Aboard at a Ship's Helm	148
An Ocean Lullaby	46
An Old Song Re-Sung	157
And God Created the Great Whales	40
Annabel Lee	23
Ballad of the Tempest	97
Beautiful Proud Sea	98
Black-Eyed Susan	135
Boats in a Fog	158
Byron's Address to the Ocean	131
Casabianca	37
Choosing a Mast	159
Cleaning Ship	95
Columbus (Miller)	2
Columbus (Nash)	147
Crossing the Bar	20
Deep Calleth Unto Deep	107
Dover Beach	149
Down Among the Wharves	55
Drinking Song	63
Epitaph for a Sailor Buried Ashore	61
Exiled	30
Father Mapple's Hymn from Moby Dick	41
Hell's Pavement	94
Hurrah for the Sea	53
If I Could Grasp a Wave from the Great Sea	21
Is My Lover on the Sea?	134
Loomings from Moby Dick	4
Low-Tide	73
Mariners	36
My Bounding Bark	27
Nights on the Indian Ocean	118
Nothing Like Grog	65

O Captain! My Captain!	8
Of the Sea, A Song	124
Old Ironsides	16
Old Ship Riggers	57
Once by the Pacific	104
On the Sea	133
Psalm CVII, Verses 23-30	127
Reefing Topsails	17
Requiem	167
Rivets	69
Sailor Man	72
Sam Swipes	67
Sea Call	96
Sea-Fever	1
Shakespeare on the Sea, from Pericles	128
Ships that Pass in the Night	45
Sir Joseph's Song	151
Song from 'The Tempest'	14
Song of the Gulf Stream	115
Song of the Sea	120
Spirit of Freedom, Thou Dost Love the Sea	12
Sunrise at Sea	112
The Alarmed Skipper	140
The Beauty of the Ocean	110
The Coast of Peru	122
The Creation of the Sea	126
The Cruise of the "P.C."	39
The Deep	28
The Equinox	109
The Fisherman	22
The Fisher's Life	13
The Gulf Stream	117
The Life of a Tar	9
The Lookout	62
The Main-Sheet Song	10
The Mariners' Compass	64
The Owl and the Pussy-Cat	43
The Pacific	119
The Phantom Ship	145
The Rime of the Ancient Mariner	75
The Sailor to his Parrot	142
The Sea Gypsy	7
The Sea-King	143
The Sea-King's Burial	47

The Seaman's Life	59
The Secret of the Sea (Longfellow)	25
The Secret of the Sea (Phillips)	129
The Ship and Her Makers	165
The Ship of State	29
The Shipwreck	113
The Tarry Buccaneer	164
The Tide Rises, The Tide Falls	71
The Trackless Deeps	125
The Walloping Window-Blind	32
The Whale	42
The Walrus and the Carpenter	153
The Wreck of the Hesperus	99
They Who Possess the Sea	44
Thornton Beach	106
Tides	102
To the Harbormaster	161
To the Humpback Whales	105
Unfathomable Sea!	34
Where is the Sea?	52
Where Lies the Land?	74

INDEX OF AUTHORS

Adams, Marguerite Janvrin	
They Who Possess the Sea	44
Anonymous	
Hurrah for the Sea	53
My Bounding Bark	27
The Coast of Peru	122
The Cruise of the "P.C."	39
The Fisher's Life	13
The Life of a Tar	9
The Mariners' Compass	64
The Seaman's Life	59
The Whale	42
Arnold, Matthew	
Dover Beach	149
Bailey, H. Sewall	
Sailor Man	72
Bellamann, Henry	
The Gulf Stream	117

Brainard, John G.C.
    The Deep   28
Brown, Abbie Farwell
    The Fisherman   22
Burton, Richard
    Song of the Sea   120
Byron, Lord (George Gordon)
    Byron's Address to the Ocean   131
Campbell, Roy
    Choosing a Mast   159
Carroll, Lewis
    The Walrus and the Carpenter   153
Carryl, Charles E.
    The Walloping Window-Blind   32
Clough, Arthur Hugh
    Where Lies the Land?   74
Cody, H.A.
    Old Ship Riggers   57
Coleridge, Samuel Taylor
    The Rime of the Ancient Mariner   75
Collins, William
    The Lookout   62
Cornwall, Barry
    Is My Lover on the Sea?   134
Cunningham, Allan
    A Wet Sheet and a Flowing Sea   6
Davies, W.H.
    The Sailor to his Parrot   142
Day, Thomas Fleming
    The Main-Sheet Song   10
Dibdin, Charles
    Nothing Like Grog   65
Dodge, Henry Nehemiah
    Deep Calleth Unto Deep   107
    Spirit of Freedom, Thou Dost Love the Sea   12
Fielder, E.A.
    Of the Sea, A Song   124
Fields, James T.
    Ballad of the Tempest   97
    The Alarmed Skipper   140
Ford, Francis Alan
    Song of the Gulf Stream   115
Frost, Robert
    Once by the Pacific   104

Gay, John
    Black-Eyed Susan 135
Gilbert, W.S.
    Sir Joseph's Song 151
Grant, Percy Stickney
    The Pacific 119
Harris, Hazel Harper
    A Sailor's Song 15
Hemans, Felicia
    Casabianca 37
    Where is the Sea? 52
Holmes, Oliver Wendell
    Old Ironsides 16
Hovey, Richard
    The Sea Gypsy 7
Jeffers, Robinson
    Boats in a Fog 158
Jewett, Eleanore Myers
    Down Among the Wharves 55
Keats, John
    On the Sea 133
Keeler, Charles
    An Ocean Lullaby 46
    Cleaning Ship 95
Lear, Edward
    The Owl and the Pussy-Cat 43
Longfellow, Henry Wadsworth
    Ships That Pass in the Night 45
    The Equinox 109
    The Phantom Ship 145
    The Secret of the Sea 25
    The Ship of State 29
    The Tide Rises, The Tide Falls 71
    The Wreck of the Hesperus 99
McClure, Michael
    Thornton Beach 106
Mackay, Charles
    The Sea-King's Burial 47
Marryat, Frederick
    Drinking Song 63
    Sam Swipes 67
Masefield, John
    An Old Song Re-Sung 157
    A Valediction 162

A Wanderer's Song 163
Hell's Pavement 94
Sea-Fever 1
The Ship and Her Makers 165
The Tarry Buccaneer 164
Melville, Horman
Father Mapple's Hymn 41
Loomings 4
Millay, Edna St. Vincent
Exiled 30
Low-Tide 73
Miller, Joaquin
Columbus 2
Milton, John
And God Created the Great Whales 40
The Creation of the Sea 126
Mitchell, Walter
Reefing Topsails 17
Moreland, John Richard
If I Could Grasp a Wave from the Great Sea 21
Morowitz, Harold J.
To the Humpback Whales 105
Morton, David
Mariners 36
Nash, Ogden
Columbus 147
O'Hara, Frank
To the Harbormaster 161
Olds, N.S.
Rivets 69
Palmer, E.H.
The Shipwreck 113
Phillips, Susan K
The Secret of the Sea 129
Poe, Edgar Allan
Annabel Lee 23
Prys-Jones, A.G.
Tides 102
Rice, Cale Young
Nights on the Indian Ocean 118
Roberts, Charles G.D.
Epitaph for a Sailor Buried Ashore 61
Roche, J.J.
A Sailor's Yarn 137

Sargent, Epes
    A Life on the Ocean Wave   *5*
Shakespeare, William
    A Sea Dirge   *35*
    Shakespeare on the Sea   *128*
    Song from The 'Tempest'   *11*
Shelly, Percy Bysshe
    The Trackless Deeps   *125*
    Unfathomable Sea!   *34*
Stevenson, Robert Louis
    Requiem   *167*
Swinburne, Algernon Charles
    Sunrise at Sea   *112*
Teasdale, Sara
    Beautiful Proud Sea   *98*
Tennyson, Alfred
    Crossing the Bar   *20*
Tooker, L. Frank
    The Sea-King   *143*
Walker, Thomas M.
    The Beauty of the Ocean   *110*
Whitman, Walt
    Aboard at a Ship's Helm   *148*
    O Captain! My Captain!   *8*
Widdemer, Margaret
    Sea Call   *96*